"In his latest gem, *Northern Magic*, Edred Thorsson opens up a completely new area of Nordic magical lore, and as well, that of the Vikings. Here he ably explains the differences between 'Seidr' and 'Galdr' and includes in-depth explanations and analyses of the meaning of the Viking Futhark runes as distinct from the better known common Germanic ones. Practical training is offered in constructing Viking Galdor stafen for the first time ever. One is instructed how to obtain communication with one's 'fetch animal.' Furthermore, Edred introduces the old Germanic 'Hexcraeft,' better known in the U.S. as 'Pennsylvanian Dutch'; this section is a crash course in practical magic in itself. The last section in this book is devoted to a discussion of the Germanic Renaissance in the most forthright and courageous manner ever. This book, more than any of his others, is written with real feeling as well as with his usual intelligence and therefore is appealing to both mind and heart. It can no longer be denied that Edred Thorsson is the leading Adept in the Germanic Mysteries."

—**Freya Aswynn**
author of *Leaves of Yggdrasil*

"This book is a concise presentation of the most essential elements of Edred Thorsson's many years of work within the Teutonic tradition. In this work, Thorsson combines living folk tradition with ancient lore and scholarship with magical experience to bring forth the secret wisdom of our Northern ancestors in a practical and accessible form. A worthy successor to *Futhark* and *Runelore!*"

—**Kveldulf Gundarsson**
author of *Teutonic Magic*

About the Author

Edred Thorsson is well known as the author of such books as *Futhark: A Handbook of Rune Magic, Runelore: A Handbook of Esoteric Runology, At the Well of Wyrd: A Handbook of Runic Divination, Rune-Might,* and *A Book of Troth.* Since 1972, he has been dedicated to the esoteric and exoteric study of the Indo-European religion and culture at major universities in Germany and in the U.S. *Northern Magic* represents a practical exploration of many topics in the field of Germanic magic.

To Write to the Author

We cannot guarantee that every letter written to the author can be answered, but all will be forwarded. Both the author and the publisher appreciate hearing from readers, learning of your enjoyment and benefit from this book. Llewellyn also publishes a bi-monthly news magazine with news and reviews of practical esoteric studies and articles helpful to the student, and some readers' questions and comments to the author may be answered through this magazine's columns if permission to do so is included in the original letter. The author sometimes participates in seminars and workshops, and dates and places are announced in *The Llewellyn New Times.* To write to the author, or to ask a question, write to:

Edred Thorsson
c/o THE LLEWELLYN NEW TIMES
P.O. Box 64383-782, St. Paul, MN 55164-0383, U.S.A.
For a reply, please enclose a self-addressed, stamped
envelope or an international reply coupon for addresses
outside of the U.S.A., or enclose $1.00 to cover costs.

Llewellyn's World Magic Series

Northern Magic

Mysteries of the Norse, Germans & English

Edred Thorsson

1992
Llewellyn Publications
St. Paul, Minnesota 55164-0383, U.S.A.

First Edition
First Printing, 1992

Cover painting by Lissanne Lake

Library of Congress Cataloging-in-Publication Data
    Northern Magic : mysteries of the Norse, Germans & English / Edred Thorsson.
        p. cm. — (Llewellyn's world magic series)
    Includes bibliographical references.
    ISBN 0-87542-782-0 : $4.95
    1. Magic, Germanic. I. Title. II. Series.
BF1622.G3T483   1991   91-40521
133.4'3'0943—dc20   CIP

Llewellyn Publications
A Division of Llewellyn Worldwide, Ltd.
P.O. Box 64383, St. Paul, MN 55164-0383

LLEWELLYN'S WORLD MAGIC SERIES

At the core of every religion, at the foundation of every culture, there is MAGIC.

Magic sees the World as *alive,* as the home which humanity shares with beings and powers both visible and invisible with whom and which we can *interface* to either our advantage or disadvantage—depending upon our awareness and intention.

Religious worship and communion is one kind of magic, and just as there are many religions in the world so are there many magical systems.

Religion, and magic, are ways of seeing and relating to the *creative* powers, the *living* energies, the *all-pervading* spirit, the *underlying* intelligence that is the universe within which we and all else exist.

Neither Religion nor Magic conflict with Science. All share the same goals and the same limitations: always seeking Truth, forever haunted by human limitations in perceiving that truth. Magic is "technology" based upon experience and *extrasensory insight,* providing its practitioners with methods of greater influence and control over the world of the invisible before it impinges on the world of the visible.

The study of world magic not only enhances your understanding of the world in which you live, and hence your ability to *live better,* but brings you into touch with the *inner essence* of your long evolutionary heritage and most particularly—as in the case of the magical system identified most closely with your forebears—with *the archetypal images and forces most alive in your whole consciousness.*

Also by Edred Thorsson

Futhark: A Handbook of Rune Magic
Runelore: A Handbook of Esoteric Runology
At the Well of Wyrd:
  A Handbook of Runic Divination
The Truth About Teutonic Magick
A Book of Troth
Rune Might
The Nine Doors of Midgard

As S. Edred Flowers
Fire and Ice

CONTENTS

Abbreviations

B.C.E.   Before the Common Era (= B.C.)
C.E.   Common Era (= A.D.)
Ice.   Icelandic
ON   Old Norse

Introduction

High within a towering building in a major urban city a modern runemaster carves his will upon the very warp and woof of the universal fabric. He carves the elder signs and sings the ancient rune songs. In doing this he becomes one with the patterns laid down by his ancestors in centuries before. In learning the lore and using it actively the modern magician makes remanifest the eternal runes which inform a timeless process of becoming. The modern runemaster, like his ancestors, gladly rides the waves of cosmic flux and guides his ship across a sea of eternal becoming. From his tower, whether it is the crags of the ancient *Externsteine* or the modern high-rise apartment, the runemasters of all ages have held the secret of altering the fabric of the world—this is as true today as it was two thousand years ago.

We live in an age where that which is *holistic* and *natural* is understood and sought more than ever. People want to live in harmony with nature, to understand the unity of the "body-mind-spirit." These are all noble and valuable goals. The pathway to these goals has, however, been severely obstructed. The blockages come from within; the keys to unblocking these pathways must also come from within. But, as we so often see in this universe, the *secret*—**the Rune**

—to their liberation has come from without—from the runic realm of Valhalla itself standing beyond the limits of nature.

If you are interested in living a *whole*-istic life in which the integration or unity of body-mind-spirit is gained and understood, it should be obvious that a key to knowledge concerning your spiritual heritage is to be found in the "heritage" of your body—in the "genetic code" which you have inherited from your distant ancestors. Thus your own most natural, most intuitive path is an *ancestral* path.

We in the "west" have often made idealized models out of other (exotic) cultural traditions: the American Indians, the Indians of Asia, and even the Afro-Caribbean, just to name a few. What we have idealized is their great sense of continuous tradition and their deep level of spiritual authenticity. If we want this for ourselves—individually or collectively—we must find it *within ourselves*. It cannot be truly gained from sources outside our tradition of body-mind-spirit unity. We can learn a great deal from other traditions—but from a *holistic* viewpoint they remain something outside ourselves.

I remember when I was about six years old on a trip to New Mexico and Arizona that I cried myself to sleep one night wishing that I had been "born an Indian." I was so struck by *something* about these noble, authentic, and self-aware people. But what my six year old mind could not understand was that it was not the Indians as such that I found so inspiring but it was the things which they represented and embodied for *themselves.* If you want to (re-)capture the loss of nobility, authenticity and self-awareness that the American Indians or other traditional peoples have you cannot recover it from them—you must recover it from within your own being and self.

A large part of Teutonic, or Runic, Magic is developing the techniques to recover our authentic individual and collective souls from the depths of Hel (the dead) and the heights of Asgardhr (the eternally yet transcendently living). High Runic Magic is a cosmic level Working for the recovery of our lost souls, and for the transformation of our world according to the timeless structure of those souls. When you participate fully in Runic Magic you are to some extent participating in this cosmic level of "shamanic magic."

In this primer of the magic of the Northern way you will be introduced to the major concepts and practices of Gothic or Germanic Magic.

Before true and deep success can be expected in this kind of magic, a basic understanding of the world, of the macrocosm, and of the true nature of the body/soul complex, or microcosm, should be gained. The true Teutonic magician will want to know and understand the Gods and Goddesses who populate the pantheon of the timeless realms beyond Midgard.

After such knowledge is gained, the magician can move on to the actual practice of galdor and seith These are the two technical forms of "magic" the reader meet in this book. Galdor mainly uses runes and incantations or meta-linguistic formulas (such as poetry or *"mantras"*) to effect the will of the magician. Seith, on the other hand, is closely related to shamanism and involves the induction of trance states and traversing of the various realms of reality throughout the structure of the World-Tree, Yggdrasill.

It is also important to note that the Germanic, or Northern, tradition has had a profound effect on the shape of what is commonly called the Western tradition. The reasons for this will also be explored in the following pages. In addition to that historical aspect, I will also give some overview of the rebirth of the Northern tradition from the time of its "official" demise at the end of the so-called Viking Age to the most recent attempts to reawaken to the call of our ancient magics and to the songs of our elder faith.

For those already experienced in runic and other forms of Teutonic magic, this book also has a great deal which is new and unique to offer. Here you will be given what are perhaps the most exact instructions yet printed of how to perform "Pennsylvania Dutch" Hex-Magic, or the practical keys to working with the Icelandic magical signs *(galdrastafir)* so often referred to in historical and theoretical books.

1 The Teutons Today

From ancient times the Teutons have been known as a group of people who speak the Germanic group of languages. Some prefer the term "Teutonic" over "Germanic" to avoid the confusion between the words "Germanic" and "German." But in reality the terms "Teutonic" and "Germanic" mean the same thing. The term "Gothic" has even been applied to the whole of the Germanic realm, although this too originally referred to only one branch of the Germanic family. Today any of these three terms, Germanic, Teutonic, or Gothic, may refer to the overall tradition of this original group. The English, German, Dutch, Icelandic, Danish, Norwegian, and Swedish peoples are all directly descended from this ancient Germanic cultural stock. It is also important to realize that they left their indelible mark on the cultures of the French, Spanish, and Italian nations, as they founded the first true states in those lands after the fall of the Roman Empire.

The Ostrogoths and Longobards (in Lombardy, northern Italy) founded early medieval kingdoms in Italy. The Visigoths formed kingdoms in southern France and in Spain. There was also an early Swabian kingdom in Spain. The region in southern Spain known as Andalusia is derived from the name of the Germanic people who set up a medieval kingdom there, the Vandals. (The original name was Vandalusia.) The Franks eventually settled in what is now northern France—and it is from the name of this tribe that the name of the country is derived. In all of these instances the Germanic tribes gave a sense of national identity to the regions in question after the destruction of the Roman Empire.

The Teutons not only had a tradition of religion and mythology unique to themselves, although closely related to their other Indo-European brethren (Celts, Slavs, Romans, Greeks, Persians, and Indians), but they also had a unique magical system which has survived in various forms—most notably rune magic.

The magical and religious teachings of these people are most clearly laid out in the ancient texts known as the *Eddas* of which there is a younger, or prose version, and an elder, or poetic version. In these works are encoded the mysteries of the Teutonic peoples. These can be understood on many levels.

In the elder days there were many more sources of the tradition, but the Christian missionaries destroyed many of them. The chief target of their hatred seems to have been the teachings and traditions surrounding the Goddess Freyja, whose poetry and songs (many of them eroto-magical) were singled out for utter obliteration.

The traditions which survived the best were those connected to the god Woden, whose loyalists were to be found in the Germanic royal houses— somewhat insulated from the influences of the new religion. This circumstance is somewhat responsible for the misguided assumption that the Teutonic tradition is a male-dominated one. This is not especially true; it is just a matter of what has been able to survive in the written tra- dition. Now is the time to revive fully the elder ways of the goddess Freyja.

In modern times the Gothic stream of magic has been largely ignored in the great magical revival in the Western world. There were revivals of the Germanic tradition in the 1500s and 1600s in Sweden, and in the late 1800s and early 1900s in Germany, but only in the past 20 years or so have there been any worldwide attempts at the revival of the ancient ways of the Teutons. At pre- sent there are many groups in the United States and Europe engaged in the work of revivifying the elder traditions of the Teutonic folk.

The practice of the Germanic forms of magic is the birthright of most readers of this book by virtue of the fact that they have been born into the life-stream of an English-speaking (Teutonic) nation. This is your most natural organic tradi- tion to deal with magically. You already "speak its language" in the most literal sense.

2 The Northern Magician

As there are several distinct kinds of Teutonic magic, so too are there several distinct kinds of Teutonic "magicians." The first kind is not really a magician in the strictest sense, but rather a priest or priestess. This is the Elder of the Troth, sometimes also known by the Old Norse terms *godhi* [goh-<u>thee</u>] or *gydhja* [<u>gith</u>-ya], for the male and female respectively. The other two kinds of magicians in the narrower sense, those who seek not only to maintain or restore the sacred order of the universe but who may also seek to make changes in it in accordance with their own wills, are the practitioners of *galdor* and *seith* [sythe]. Both may be known by the general Old Norse term *vitki,* meaning "wise one."

Whether for religious or magical purposes the practitioner of the true Northern way must undergo a period of preparation before the right pathways can be followed. This preparation comes in two forms. First the would-be *vitki* must steep him or herself in the lore of the Teutons. The mythology, legends and lore—the cosmologies and theologies—should be learned so that "thinking in" them is virtually natural. For those interested in becoming runemasters the runic tradition must also be treated in a similar way. This provides a traditional "inner landscape" for further work. It is authentic and accurate so work done within it cannot lead you astray but rather to further insight. The second part of the aspiring *vitki's* preparation can be undertaken simultaneously with the first. This is basic training in concentration and visualization. This latter element is common to success in any form of magic. However, one of the main elements of current Northern magic is the will to link the self with the higher principles of the folk-soul. For this purpose to be fulfilled, the first element is absolutely essential.

The Northern magician or *vitki* is a very independent sort. In ancient times as well as today many prefer to work alone or in very small groups, loosely affiliated within a guild. (This is not so for the true religious tradition which seeks to involve the whole community.) The independence of the Teutonic magician goes beyond the social aspect and is also exemplified in his or her magical character. The *vitki* —and especially the runemaster—does not normally seek the magical aid of forces outside himself, but rather seeks to influence the course of events directly. The standard of the medieval magician evoking and coercing angels or demons to do his bidding by the power of supposedly higher forces outside himself is almost totally foreign to the Northern way of working magic.

The God and Goddess of Magic

The Teutonic magician most typically identifies him or herself with one of the major divinities of magic. This is done both for initiatory purposes —that is the god or goddess serves as a model for the development of the personality or self of the magician—and for the purpose of more effectively carrying out acts of magic. The two major godforms for this purpose are the god Woden, or Odin, and the goddess Freia, or Freyja.

Woden is the major god of galdor and of the runes and rune magic. To follow the path of Woden is to delve deeply into the mysteries (runes) of the mind and spirit, to explore without restrictions the mysteries and dark corners of life and death. The true Odinist—that is, one who follows the particular path outlined by the character of the living god Woden—is a person who seeks to understand the deepest cosmic mysteries and then to put these mysteries into a communicable form to be expressed in the world at large. This is part of doing the Work of Woden. The path of Odin is one which combines the intellectual with the intuitive—but which in both cases strives toward the objectively real and powerful. The highest aim of the Odinist is self-transformation—according to the mysto-magical model provided by Odin. The true Odinist is often a loner and may be generally aloof from society, but is one who nevertheless always appreciates the need for a common traditional grounding in the myth and lore of the folk.

Freyja is the major goddess of the magic known as seith (Old Norse *seidhr*). This, for want of a better explanation, may be compared to a form of Norse shamanism. The mythology relates that Freyja taught this kind of magic to Odin (*Ynglinga saga* chapter 7). To follow the path of Freyja is to delve deeply into the mysteries of nature and of the hidden worlds which lie beneath or behind nature. The true devotee of Freyja—that is, one who follows the particular path outlined by the character of the living goddess Freyja—is a person who seeks to experience the deepest mysteries of not only the mind but of the flesh also. The path of Freyja is one which links the intuitive with physical sensations—but which in either case strives toward the direct experience of reality. This experience may, however, be expressed in highly individualized ways. Those who follow the way of the goddess Freyja often love good company and fellowship, but they just as often hold unique views that clearly separate them from the bulk of society.

The ways of Ódhinn and Freyja have a great deal in common. There are important distinctions which must be experienced to be fully understood. It is generally found that men who follow a magical path in the Germanic tradition seek to emulate Ódhinn, while women seek to emulate the way of Freyja. Religiously there is also a path of worship of the opposite wherein a male magician worships the image of Freyja, while the female magician worships that of Ódhinn. (By the way, the word "worship" is being used here in its literal and true sense of "to give honor to" someone or something and does not necessarily carry a sense of submission.)

These are just two of the more common paths for the Gothic magician to follow. To find the right path for yourself you should explore the mythology and lore of the Teutons deeply and find the image or path which most definitely resonates with the essence of your being.

3 The Northern Ways

Many are the paths leading to and from the hyperborean realms. The ancient Greeks ascribed special spiritual powers to the Northern sky and the Northern lands, as did all of the European and Indo-European peoples. It is the Germanic, Teutonic, or Gothic folk who most embody the qualities ascribed to the Northern realms.

Although it is almost impossible to describe or outline the vast complexity of aspects which go into making up the magical traditions and mysteries we call the Northern Way, it is possible to give some notion of the scope of this great tradition.

The Northern Way encompasses all aspects of life and culture—or it can if you have need of it to do so. There is a whole cosmology (lore about the order of the world and how it came into being), psychology (lore about the human soul and its structure and use), theology (lore about the Gods and Goddesses or archetypes), and a whole array of magical technologies to help the *vitki* work with these concepts in productive and

healthy ways. The Germanic way can encompass
all aspects of culture, religion and social order—if
and when it is called upon to do so. This is
because its origins lay in the holistic cultural
world of the ancient Teutons. As the traditions
have come down to us, they are often fragmented.
Part of the magic is in putting these pieces back
together again in an effort to create a more holistic society and culture.

The Three Great Branches
of the Northern Way

TROTH

The first great branch of the Northern Way
is **Troth.** Troth is the way in which an explorer
on the Northern path relates to the Gods and
Goddesses and to the cultural traditions of the
folk in a true or loyal way. It is what might best
be called the religious tradition within the Northern Way. The main purpose of the Troth is to find
the right ways of doing and being, and harmoniz-
ing yourself with those ways in order to bring harmony and truth into your life.

But the troth is a somewhat free-form religion very much suited to our present day. There
are no dogmas, no holy writ, and therefore no
"heresies" possible in the true religion. It wells up
from the very flesh and blood of the members. All
individuals, all families, all clans, and all tribes
have their own unique forms of the troth.

The main technology for pursuing the troth
comes in the form of learning about the culture,
history, and mythology of your ancestors and

applying this knowledge in the form of ritual blessings performed at symbolically important times during the cycle of the year.

Learning about the culture, history, mythology of your ancestors may seem to be a purely "intellectual" exercise, but it is not just that. When you learn something about the real (not imagined) values, ideas and myths of your ancestors you take in some of them—they become part of you and have a transformative effect on your life. In ancient times this was the effect storytelling and epic recitations had on the folk. Today, in our modern (and even post-modern) age all kinds of historical data and lore (including the ancient forms) can do the work of informing us in a transformative way.

But it is not enough merely to learn about these things. If left to that level the values and principles would soon fade—if not in this life-time then in subsequent manifestations. The elder ways have survived in us precisely because the ancients applied their hidden knowledge in the form of ritual workings. This action on their part deeply encoded these messages in our very beings. In order to reawaken this knowledge and to make it manifest so that it can be handed on to subsequent generations in a conscious way, these values and myths must again be realized—made real. This is best done in ritual workings such as blessings and/or in the living your life according to a strict code of honor and loyalty to the way you have chosen for yourself within the larger troth.

This two pronged method of learning and work is the mainstay of the branch of the Northern way known as troth. It is also perhaps basic to the healthy practice of the other two branches of the Northern Way.

RUNE-GALDOR

The second great branch of the Northern Way is galdor. In one way or another galdor almost always makes use of runology on at least one level of this multi-leveled concept. Galdor is the magical technology of reshaping the (inner or outer) world in accordance with the will of the magician. Ódhinn is the master of this kind of magic, and the technique of wisdom and inspiration needed to make it work correctly.

The mainstay of the technique of galdor is revealed in the etymology of the word. It is derived from the word used to describe the sound of a raven's call—the "song of the ravens." Mythologically this is a reference to the two ravens of Ódhinn—Huginn and Muninn. These are two "voices" to which Ódhinn "listens," and from which he inquires further into mysteries. These two ravens sit on Ódhinn's shoulders and each whispers into his ear what they know. Huginn is the power of intellectual thought while Muninn is the power of reflective thought or "memory." This is a kind of memory that goes far beyond a recollection of events past. It really means the whole body of transpersonal knowledge. In the poetic Edda Ódhinn says:

> Huginn and Muninn   fly every day
> over the whole wide world;
> I dread that Huginn   will not come back.

but I fear even more for Muninn.
("Grímnismál" st. 20)

Galdor is the art and practice of first hearing, then understanding, the runic words of the ravens, and finally of putting their words to work in the world. The "ravens" are, of course, mythic codes for certain parts of the soul or psyche (see hidge and myne in chapter 4). In the center sits the self, guided by the wode (Ice. *ódhr*). It is in the oscillation between mind and memory ruled over by divine inspiration where true intelligence and wisdom arise and it is by this wisdom that the path of galdor is charted.

The aim of galdor is to make the results of this work intelligible and communicable in the objective universe—in the "real world." This is why language plays such an important role both as a symbol and as a technique in the practice of galdor. As a divinatory tool, rune-casting is the analytical method preferred by those who work galdor.

SEITH

The third great branch of the Northern Way is seith. This might be called the magical path of the body (as opposed to that of the mind). Seith originally had nothing to do with runes or runology in the strict sense, although signs and symbols of various kinds are used in conjunction with the technique these are usually not "linguistic signs." They rather "speak" directly to the unconscious mind with a minimum filter of consciousness.

Seith is also a magical technology of reshaping the (inner or outer) world in accordance with the will of the magician. Freyja rules over this kind of magic and the powers needed to make it work.

Instead of making unconscious or unknown things (runes) conscious and aware (as in galdor), the seith-worker seeks to sink into the realm of the unknown and unconscious, to become woven into it, and if need be to alter the fabric of the universe in accordance with his or her will. Seith-workers ply their magical craft mostly in the psychophysical realms of the lyke (body), hyde (shape), athem (breath) and luck *(hamingja)*. Seith makes great use of magical materials and substances such as potions, herbs and ointments.

The preferred method of divination for seith-workers is sooth-saying based on direct communication from inner realms of being, or other less analytical, more intuitive, methods of divination.

Historically the paths of galdor and seith have been used together by individuals and by various schools of Northern magic. There is nothing wrong with this—it should even be encouraged. But at the same time it is valuable for continued growth and development that the two branches be seen and understood for their differences so that nothing further is lost or "watered down."

These three great branches of the Northern or Teutonic tradition can be used in their relatively pure forms, or in any combination by the aspiring *vitki*. What is uniquely Germanic about them is their pragmatic and generally objective characters. Northern magic is result oriented. Philosophically there is also the tendency to see flux and change, or the dynamic movement between two extremes (the cosmic fire and ice) as a basically **good and desirable thing.** In the Germanic view as long as their is fluidity and flux there is life, and where there is life, freedom is possible. The final aim of the Northern mysteries is the establishment of free and independent individuals and peoples—all sovereign and authentic within themselves.

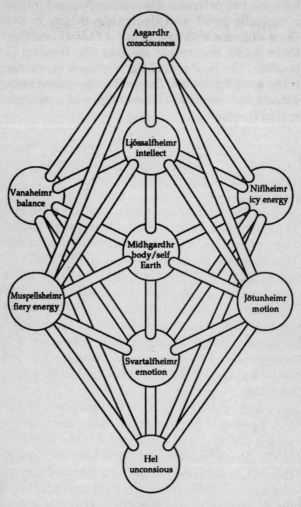

Figure 1
The Pattern of Yggdrasill

4 The Lore of the Worlds

In the Germanic vision of the universe and of humanity there have always been many dimensions or worlds. In the larger world or macrocosm this is shown by the lore about the World-Tree, Yggdrasill. This "tree" is said to be made up of nine realms or worlds. A symbolic model of Yggdrasill is shown in Figure 1. The actual arrangement of the worlds cannot really be shown in two or three dimensions. This is because it is always clear in every account that the "tree" is really a symbol of the multidimensional structure of reality.

Asgard (*Ásgardhr*) is the kingdom of the Æsir, and of those Vanir who have come to live among the Æsir. Hel is the realm of the dead and of the forces of universal dissolution. Lightelf-Home (*Ljóssálfheimr*) is the kingdom of the elves (demigods and divinized ancestral spirits). This is the dimension of the structures of the intellect. Opposite this is Swartelf-Home (*Svartálfheimr*). Swartelf is another name for dwarf. The dwarves, like the Lightelves, are essentially ancestral spirits or demigods, but dwarves are not intellectual or spiritual in character. They embody the forces in the world that give structure and shape to things. Wane-Home *(Vanaheimr)* is the realm of the Wanes or Vanir, which are further described below. Opposite this is Etin-Home *(Jötunheimr)*. This is the realm of primeval forces of blind, non-conscious chaos and/or order. An etin is a non-conscious construct. The realms of Muspell-Home *(Muspellsheimr)* and Nifel-Home *(Niflheimr)* are the realms of cosmic fire and ice, respectively. It is from these two extremes of cosmic activity, or energy/matter, that the universe comes into being. Between and among all of these opposing forces is the realm of all-potential, the blessed land of Midgard *(Midhgardhr)*—the enclosure in the midst of all. In this Middle-Earth lives humankind, the only other being in the cosmos which fully shares (potentially) the gift of consciousness with the Gods and Goddesses.

The Soul

The mythic tradition of the Teutons tells us that the first man and woman were formed from trees by the triadic Gods of consciousness (Woden-Willi-Weh or Ódhinn-Hœnir-Lódhurr). The man was made from an ash tree, the woman from an elm. In the poetry of the North, human beings are often referred to as trees; for example, a warrior will be called "the oak of battle." This points to the essential link between the idea of the tree on the cosmic scale (Yggdrasill) and the tree on the individual human scale. The multi-dimensional pattern of existence found in the Yggdrasill model is also present in the essence of the human being.

It is meaningful in the lore of the North that humans were made from already living and organic life—not from dead earth.

The *Poetic Edda* tells us (in the "Völuspá" st. 18) that Woden, Willi, and Weh formed the original man and woman by giving to them certain gifts:

> Athem they had not, wode they had not.
> being nor bearing, nor blooming hue;
> athem gave Ódhinn Hœnir gave wode,
> being, Lódhurr, and blooming hue.

So in the Germanic tradition the human being is made up of a complex of essences, powers—or, if you will, **souls.** All of these come together in a certain place and time to give shape to a unique human manifestation. But some of these qualities or essences may pre-exist a person's present manifestation or "incarnation." At the same time these qualities or powers may indeed live on after the present manifestation or incarnation has come to an end.

By the same token the truth about the human being is something much more than we can readily see. The ancient Teutons had dozens of terms for various aspects of the human body and soul. Each one of these was used with a technical accuracy that would put a modern psychologist to shame. Speakers of languages have many terms for the fine distinctions between and among things that they know well. Eskimos may have 15 words for "white" because they are able to make fine distinctions among the fine gradations of color in their "all white" world. All we might see or be able to talk about would be "white." The Eskimos live in an "all white" world in which they are able to make fine distinctions because they are so familiar with it. The same can be said for our ancestors, who perhaps lived in a more spiritual world—as evidenced by their many words for spiritual concepts.

According to Germanic tradition the individual human being is really a body-soul, or psychosomatic complex. The body and its appearance are aspects of this, as are the breath (athem), the inspiration (wode), the mind, the memory (personal as well as collective), the heart, the will, and certain magical faculties which individuals may or may not have acquired. Individuals may have more than one of some of these magical faculties—such as the *hamingja*, which is the repository of personal luck or fortune. Acquiring these magical bodies or the strengthening of them is one of the main tasks of the Northern Way. All exercise of the will and of consciousness increases this power.

Because the psyche or soul and the cosmos or world are both symbolically seen as trees in the Northern tradition, we can speak of a Germanic teaching of a "psychocosmolgy." This teaches the way of the linkages between the soul and the world. If the inner world of the soul is explored and understood, the gateways are opened to a greater understanding of the larger world. The

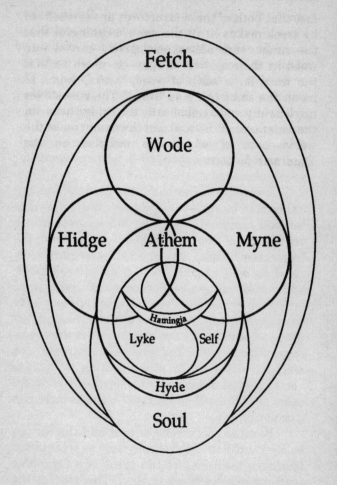

Figure 2
The Map of the Soul

fact that both of these structures are symbolized by trees makes it all the more meaningful that the runes were almost exclusively carved into wood in their earliest usages—so much so that the word for a stick of wood, "stave," came to mean the same thing as "rune." The runestaves are literally and symbolically the bridge between the inner tree of the soul and the outer tree of the world—both of which are modeled on the Yggdrasill pattern.

5 The Gods and Goddesses

The Gods and Goddesses of the North are not dead and forgotten forms. As long as their folk, their actual descendants, live in flesh and blood in Midgard, their being will be present. They are not dead, merely forgotten by most of their folk. They only await their true remembering to reawaken them in the hearts and minds of their folk.

Anyone seeking along the Northern Way has access to a great wealth of divine living archetypes. These Gods and Goddesses can be approached in many ways. Perhaps the first way is through absorbing the lore and myths of the Teutonic folk, then through vision-quests, the performance of blessings (religious rites), and magical calls to the Gods and Goddesses.

The picture of the divine family among the Teutonic folk groups and their mythologies is at once more complicated than it might at first appear and yet at the same time quite simple. The complexity comes from the fact that there is not a single unified pan-Germanic mythology as such. There are at least four great branches of the tradition: the Northern branch (Scandinavian), the Western branch (Anglo-Saxon), the Southern branch (German), and the Eastern branch (Gothic). Each one shares somewhat in the mythology of the other, but each has its own distinct form as well. The problem is that only the Northern branch has preserved a true body of original mythological material—the *Eddas*. The other branches are in fragments.

But from a real working standpoint this situation is not so bad. This is because, although myths may be helpful in illustrating the qualities of the various divinities and may provide some material for ritual structures, they are not the whole of the religion. After all, one can still practice Christianity or Judaism without the Bible— how many good Christians or Jews have actually read their corpus of mythological texts?

Finally, what makes the situation much simpler than it might at first appear is the fact that only a small group of the Germanic divinities were ever the objects of widespread public or official cults. This fact, and the identity of those divinities, is easily established by looking at maps of that part of northern Europe. The old cult-sites of the major divinities usually preserve the name and nature of the site. Whether it is Wanborough in England, or Godesberg in Germany (both of which mean "hill of Woden"), or whether it is Torslev (Thorr's field) in Denmark or Torso (Thorr's island) in Sweden, or whether it is Froihov (Freyja's temple) in Norway or Frotuna (Freyja's enclosure) in Sweden, it is quite easy to see which Gods and Goddesses of the North were the objects of widespread and public worship in ancient times.

There are many other Gods and Goddesses, of course, but these are either divinities for highly specialized or institutional functions, or they are reserved for household religious activities only. This last group quite often comes in groups, such as the elves, dises, dwarves, and so forth. Finally there are those divinities who seem to have a purely mythological or even cosmological function. These may be quite important, such as Baldur, but nevertheless they were never the object of a religious cult in the sense we would normally think of it.

There is a whole pantheon of Northern Gods and Goddesses. This pantheon, or "family," of divine forms gives the individual a pattern of archetypes which embody the whole of human experience and potential. All who are interested in seriously pursuing the Northern Way will make themselves familiar with the Gods and Goddesses of the North and their mythology.

The structure or pantheon of the Gods is divided into three parts. All three are absolutely necessary to the whole. Each of the three parts has its function or characteristic work to do for the well-being of the whole. These levels are usually talked about in terms of a hierarchy. The first function is that of judgment, rationality, law, and measurement (embodied by Tiw/Týr) and of inspiration, intuition, and transformation (embodied by Woden/Ódhinn). These two together form the sovereign and intellectual part of the world and of

the human being—consciousness. They are the
Gods of the ancient kings, judges, poets, and
magicians. The second function is that of strength
(usually physical), power, and activity (embodied
by Thunar/Thórr). He and his kind are the Gods
of the warriors. The third function is that of production, regeneration. well-being, physical health
and the cycles of nature (embodied most directly
in the Lord and Lady—Freyr and Freyja). These
are the Vanir—the Gods and Goddesses of the
farmers, craftsmen, and producers of all kinds.
But the Vanir also have their magic, and all farmers could also be warriors. So in this third group
there is also a whole system unto itself—the Way
of the Vanir or *true* Wicca.

As a hierarchy these functions can be illus-
trated as in Figure 3.

This diagram helps our rational (Tyric)
minds comprehend the relationships among the
major Gods and Goddesses of the Northern
mythology. This has its validity and should be
understood by anyone interested in the Northern
Way. But there is another way of looking at it
which may be more Odinic (and more Freyic).
Each of the three parts are segments of a whole
arranged in a circle or within a ring.

These three segments of the pantheon were
in ancient times identified with emblematic colors. This color symbolism surely varied somewhat
from tribe to tribe and region to region. In the
"Rígsthula" in the *Poetic Edda,* for example, we
see that the first group has white as its color, the
second group is red, and the third group is black.

An alternate system would be to refer to the

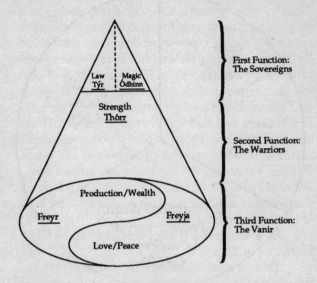

Figure 3
The Functions of the Germanic Pantheon

groups not by numbers but by colors. Perhaps also the colors white for the Tyric function, blue for the Odinic, red for the Thoric, and green for the Vanic (Freyr and Freyja) would be more suitable, as indicated in on the next page in Figure 4.

From a magical point of view, the chief God and Goddess on the Northern paths are Woden (known as Ódhinn in Old Norse) and Freyja. Both are powerful magical archetypes to be explored by both male and female magicians on the Teutonic paths. These are the models of consciousness that most magicians will seek to emulate in their per-

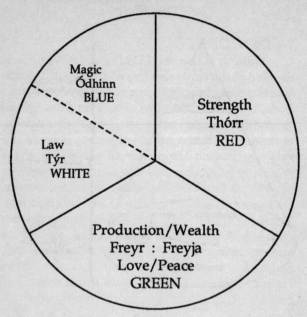

Figure 4
The Ring of the Gods and Goddesses

sonal magical developments.

There is a whole pantheon of magical archetypes with whom the *vitki* can work. The higher divinities are divided into two kinds, the Æsir and Vanir. The Æsir are the Gods and Goddesses of social order and of consciousness, while the Vanir are the divinities of nature and well-being. Especially the "magical divinities," Óðhinn and Freyja, cross over these natural boundaries at will.

The Æsir

WODEN/ÓDHINN
Ódhinn is the chief God of the *vitkar*. He is the God of the runemasters, who attempt to emulate the archetypal pattern of his myths in their lives. Ódhinn is the God who sacrifices (gives) "himself to himself" in an act of magical initiation in order to gain the runes—the knowledge of self and cosmos and the power to act within these realms, even on occasion to reshape parts of them at will. Ódhinn is the God of magic, poetry, ecstasy, and divine synthesis of consciousness. Through the pattern of this God a runemaster can gain hidden knowledge of things past and future and can reweave the warp and woof of the world. Animals attributed to Ódhinn are the eagle, ravens, wolves, the horse, and the serpent. His name written in younger runes would appear as

ᚾᚦᛁᚾ

TÍW/TYR
Tiw is the God of Law. He rules over justice and rational thought. He measures out all things in their right and proper order. Tiw is the God of true Troth and can always be trusted. His name is the same as Zeus and Jupiter. An alternate form of Týr in certain Scandinavian regions is the God Ullr or Ullinn. His name written in younger runes would appear as ᛏᛁᛣ

THUNAR / THORR

The name Thunar means the thunderer. Thunar is the God of steadfast loyalty and troth—staunch defender of Gods and humanity. He is the warrior among the Gods. His chief weapon is Mjöllnir the hammer. The animal attributed to Thunar is the goat. His name written in younger runes would appear as follows: ᚦᚢᚱ

FRIGGA / FRIGG

Frigga is also an important Goddess among the Æsir who influences the maintaining of social order within domestic existence. She is the wife of Ódhinn and is said to have great prophetic powers. But, although she has prophetic knowledge, she rarely speaks it. Her name written in younger runes would appear as ᚠᚱᛁᚴ

The Vanir

FREIA / FREYJA

Freyja is the Goddess of magic, eroticism, and physical well-being. Freyr is Freyja's twin brother. The names Freyr and Freyja literally mean the "Lord and the Lady." Her chief kind of magic is seith. This usually involves trance induction and may also involve travel between and among the various worlds of Yggdrasill. She also controls the powers of the natural cycles—for which her magical necklace, the Brisingamen, is a symbol. Animals attributed to her include the sow and cats. Her name written in younger runes would appear as ᚠᚱᛅᛁᛅ

FREI / FREYR

Freyr is the lord of prosperity, material and physical well-being, peace (frith), and eroticism. He is said to be the *veraldargodh*—the God of the World. He controls the natural processes in the land and in the air over the land. Animals attributed to him are the horse, the boar and the deer or stag. His name written in younger runes would appear as ᚠᚱᛅᛁᛦ

The kind of religion and magic practiced under the auspices of "the Lord and Lady" in ancient Anglo-Saxon England was that which first was called by the Old English or Anglo-Saxon word: *wiccecræft* [witchuh-craft].

NJORTH / NJÖRDHR

Another important Vanic God is Njördhr. He is the father of Freyja and Freyr. Njördhr is the lord of material well-being and abundance. He controls the natural processes in the sea and in the air over the sea. His name written in younger runes would appear as ᚾᛁᛅᚢᚦᛦ

There are other Gods and Goddesses to be explored if you set out on the Northern way. But the ones already mentioned here are the **key** deities who open the ways to the divine realms. These are the main deities to whom gifts are normally given.

The names of other Gods and Goddesses can

also be used in magical workings for very specific magical aims. Some of the techniques for using the names can be learned in the seventh and eighth chapters of this book.

Some of the other Gods and Goddesses named by Snorri Sturluson in his *Edda* are:

Bragi (ᛒᚱᛆᚴᛁ): The God of Eloquence; wisdom and poetry are also in his domain. He is the husband of Idhunn.

Eir (ᛂᛁᚱ): Goddess of Healing. She is the physician of the Gods and Goddesses.

Forseti (ᚠᚢᚱᛌᛂᛏᛁ): A God of Justice. He can reconcile opposing sides on any issue.

Fulla (ᚠᚢᛚᛆ): She is a loyal attendant of Frigga. She is a supporter of the Goddess—who makes it possible for the great one to do her work.

Gefjon (ᚴᛂᚠᛁᚢᚾ): Goddess of Virtue. She is the "gracious" or "giving one." From her you may obtain gifts of the body and spirit. Probably an aspect of Freyja.

Gná (ᚴᚾᛆ): Goddess of Transformation. She raises awareness to towering heights. She is a follower of Frigg.

Heimdallr (ᚼᛂᛁᛘᛏᛆᛚᚱ): The God of Guardianship. Clairvoyance and vigilance are also qualities ruled over by him.

Hlín (ᚼᛚᛁᚾ): Goddess who protects people from physical danger. She is a follower of Frigg.

Hödhr (✳⌁⋔ᛈ⋏): The God of Blind Force. He is brute strength and the embodiment of conflict.

Idhunn (⋁ᛈ⋔⋏): Goddess of eternal renewal. She helps to sustain the vigor of divine forces in the universe as the guardian of the golden apples of the Æsir.

Lofn (⌁⋔ᚠ⋏): Goddess of Indulgence. From her, permission can be granted to indulge in sexual liaisons or acts otherwise forbidden by custom or law. She is attached to both Frigg and Ódhinn.

Loki (⌁⋔ᛏ⋁): He is not fully a God, as he is of the etin-kin, but he is the "blood brother" of Ódhinn and is the companion of the Æsir. He rules over beauty and deception, cunning and guile. He is the trickster and mischief maker. Loki is powerful in laughter and humor. It is most likely that Loki is but the "shadow side" of the God Ódhinn.

Sága (ᛋ⋏ᚷ⋌): Her name means "seeress" or "speaker of prophecy." She is likely an active aspect of Frigg, and is powerful in prophetic knowledge.

Sjöfn (ᛋ⋁⋌⋔ᚠ⋌): Goddess of Love. She can be called upon to turn anyone's mind to thoughts of love.

Snotra (ᛋ⋉⋔⋔ᛉ⋌): Goddess of Intelligence.

Syn (ᛋᛁᚾ): Goddess of Denial. She is a powerful defender in legal matters in which one is accused.

Ullr (ᚢᛚᛦ): May be the same as Tyr. But Ullr expresses the aspect of Týr having more to do with precision and coordination of physical faculties and skills, such as those having to do with skiing, hunting, archery, and so forth. He is a powerful figure to invoke for battle because of the martial skill he gives.

Vali (ᚢᛅᛚᛁ): A God of Vengeance. The avenger of Baldur.

Vár (ᚢᛆᛦ): Goddess of Honesty. She takes vengeance on those who break their promises made in formal vows and contracts.

Vídharr (ᚢᛁᚦᛅᚱ): A God of Vengeance. He is the avenger of his "father" Ódhinn—of whom he is a projection. Vídharr is the God of Silence and is good for overcoming crisis.

Vör (ᚢᛅᚢᛦ): Goddess of Awareness. She is very wise, and nothing can be hidden from her insight and intuition.

These Gods and Goddesses and their names can be used in a variety of practical ways. The divinities can be invoked and gifts given to them in exchange for gifts which they are able to return to you. The techniques for this are explained in chapter 6. Their names can also be used as the basis for magical runic formulas or in the creation of bind-rune sigils as explained in chapter 8.

6 The Troth

The Northern mysteries are firmly rooted in the essence of the Germanic mythical tradition or "religion." This religion is variously known as Odinism (due mostly to the fact that Odin is the chief of the Northern Gods), as *Ásatrú* (which is an Icelandic term for the troth *[trú]* of the Gods *[Æsir]*), or simply and most straightforwardly as the Troth. The term "troth" is just a simple, direct English word that means "faith," or more exactly, *loyalty*. Those who are **true** are simply loyal to the Gods and Goddesses, to the ways, of their own ancestors.

The mainstays of the traditions of the Troth are contained in the *Poetic Edda,* the *Prose Edda,* the Icelandic sagas, and other epics of the Germanic peoples (such as the *Beowulf* of the Anglo-Saxons), as well as in the folklore of those people. For example, the folktales collected by Jacob and Wilhelm Grimm, the so-called "Grimms' Fairy Tales," can be great repositories of ancient lore.

This is a vast body of well documented evidence. From it the revivification of the elder ways was quite easy—once all the sources were collected and correctly interpreted.

Historically, the fate of the Troth was, of course, closely tied to that of other aspects of Germanic spirituality. Whereas the religious aspects tended to find their way into the literary and folkloristic expressions of the Germanic folk, the more specifically magical aspects became concealed within, and behind, the new imported magical forms from the south and east (Rome, Greece, Egypt, and the Middle East). This process of concealment and submersion of the cultural tradition, together with confusion of some of its elements, went on until fairly recent times. Beginning with the "Romantic" movement in Europe, people began to look at their own national traditions in an objective yet sympathetic way.

Although the history of the revival of the Troth can be traced all the way back to the time of its official demise at the hands of medieval evangelists and corrupt monarchies, for our exploration here it is only necessary to outline its most recent phase. At the close of the 1960s there was a worldwide upsurge of interest in the Teutonic religious traditions. In Germany old societies were renewed. In America and England new ones were formed. In England the Odinic Rite was founded, which was for a long time the chief exponent of the Teutonic Troth in the British Isles. In this country there was the Ásatrú Free Assembly, which was "decentralized" and disbanded in the mid-1980s. This was not due to a lack of interest, but rather to an overabundance of chaotic influences. As a traditional synthesis of the multi formed spirituality of the Germanic peoples there has arisen in this country a religious body known as the Ring of Troth.

The Ring of Troth, which is a legally recognized "church" in the United States, is made up of two distinct factors or elements. The first of these are the Elders or priesthood. Elders are strictly and traditionally trained according to a more or less standard curriculum in the Northern tradition. The idea of Eldership is that there is a need in the world today for living repositories of lore and traditional knowledge—not merely books. The main two functions of these people are to teach lore and to carry out traditional seasonal blessings. Elders are trained to replace the priesthood lost in the days when the folk were cut off from their roots. The other factor in the Ring of Troth is the local and independent Kindreds and their leaders. These really make up a "grass roots" movement. In olden times every man and woman at the head of a household carried out "priestly" functions. So it is, and so it should be, today. The Ring of Troth and its trained Elders stand ready to serve the movement as a whole.

It is considered the birthright of everyone who feels drawn to the Northern Troth by his or her ethnic or spiritual and cultural heritage to practice that Troth freely and rightly. The Troth was the established religion of our ancestors, and most "true folk" want to make it so again.

One of the mainstays of the Troth is the idea that there is a folk-soul; that is, that there is something most people would call "spiritual" which is inherited along genetic lines within a folk group. By some this idea is called "meta-genetics." Ultimately, "metagenetics" is simply the idea that there is something of a "spiritual path" encoded in the genetic material of any people. This spiritual path may by its very nature be the "path of least resistance" to spiritual development for any person belonging to that group.

In his essay "Wotan," C. G. Jung wrote:

> Archetypes are like riverbeds which dry up when the water deserts them, but which it can find again at any time. An archetype is like an old water-course along which the water of life has flowed for centuries, digging a deep channel for itself. The longer it has flowed in this channel the more likely it is that sooner or later the water will return to its old bed.

The Gods and Goddesses of the North are the archetypes of the folk to which they belong. For some time the riverbeds may have had only a trickle of water in them, but the floodgates stand ready to be opened. The floodgates of the life force are the part that is in our control now and forever. Of course, all human beings have the freedom to try to dig their own riverbeds—to create their own gods out of the dust of the ages. But such attempts are usually limited by the subjective imagination of the "creator."

The Wheel of the Year in the Troth

The chief way in which the elder path of the Troth is practiced and the Gods and Goddesses are honored or worshiped is through the ritual observation of a sacred cycle of the year. Someone can be said to be "true"—that is, loyal to the elder Troth—if he or she simply observes these times of the year. Things can get much more complicated and involved, of course, but this is the simple essence of the folkway of the North.

Historically the holidays were not necessarily calculated by astronomical events. Since much of the calendar was keyed to agricultural cycles—in other words to the cycles of natural or organic life tides—the holidays were usually also keyed to that reality. It was much more usual to begin the celebration of spring based on the sighting of the first robin or the first violet than on the mere astro-mechanical event of the vernal equinox. For this reason the timing of the holidays varied from tribal region to tribal region. There probably never was a universal Germanic calendar as such. But the principles underlying the cycles, their approximate arrangement, and certainly the order in which they come were a fairly set part of the tradition.

Winter Night (around October 15) is the Norse New Year which comes at the end of the old harvesting time. The forces of nature are finished expending their vital powers. It is the beginning of the time when people begin to turn inward to more spiritual things. This is the beginning of the most important religious phase of the year—the time of midwinter. Originally this festival, like many of the others, was actually several nights long; hence the Icelandic name for this time: *Vetrnætr*—Winter Nights

Yule (from about December 20 to December 31) is a whole period of time—the old "Yule-tide," also remembered as the "twelve days of Christmas." In this time the whole of the year is magically contained; out of it the year is regenerated from its own depths. The Yule-tide begins on Mother Night and ends on Yule itself, twelve nights from the Mother Night. This is the time when the walls between the realm of the Gods and Goddesses as well as the other worlds outside Midgard and the realm of Midgard itself become quite thin. It is a prime time to make contact with dead ancestors or the Gods—but, because the true experience of this is as often as not quite frightening for most individuals, it was not uncommon for people to stay indoors for the entire twelve nights of Yule-Tide.

Disting (around February 14) heralds the beginning of the return of the vital forces that had turned inward at the time of Winter Night. It is the time when many local assemblies are held. This festival was especially popular in ancient Sweden. This is also a time when the ground is being made ready for the planting of new seed. It is a time of preparation for things to come.

Easter (Vernal Equinox) is the full manifestation of the return of the vital powers of nature. The name of this celebration was always Teutonic. Eostre is the Goddess of the spring and of the dawn. Her name is recorded both among the Germans (among whom she is known as Ostara) and the Anglo-Saxons, from whom we, of course, get

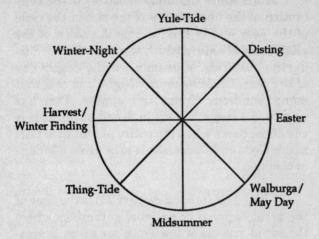

The Wheel of the Holy Year

our own English word, "Easter." It is simply one of those names the evangelists could not obliterate.

Walburga/May-Day (the night of April 30 and May 1) is a twofold affair. The night of April 30 is traditionally the night of the "witches" in central Europe. It is a time when the mysterious nightside of life is strongly manifest. The name "Walburga" probably goes back to a name of a Goddess or deified seeress—as the name literally means "Enclosure of the Fallen, or Dead." On the other hand, May Day is quite the opposite, being a bright and sunlit celebration of the dayside of life—of play and of work. Maypoles may be erected on this day, or on Midsummer Day, or both. It is for this reason that May Day is considered a workers' holiday in Europe.

Midsummer (Summer Solstice) is the celebration of the final victory of the sun in the cycle of the year and of the full manifestation of the vital forces of nature which were given birth during the Yule-Tide. Midsummer is the longest day of the year. On Midsummer Night it is said that many wondrous things can appear. This has remained a major holiday in Scandinavia. This is one of the times when the entire pantheon of Germanic Gods and Goddesses is to be given offerings in common.

Thing-tide (around August 23) is the time of the great regional or national gatherings where the social aspects of the Troth are given expression. This is the time when legislative and business matters of all kinds are attended to and when there is a great celebration of the social and organizational aspects of the Troth.

Harvest/Winter Finding (Autumnal Equinox) is the beginning of the culmination of the natural cycle of things which come into being and pass away toward new beginnings. The end of this period is celebrated on the Winter Night. bringing the cycle to a close. This is one of the major holidays—along with Midsummer and Yule.

It would be a mistake to see this cycle as one simply having to do with the cycles of "nature" in the narrower sense—in fact the mysteries of anything that comes into being and grows according to cyclical laws are contained in this pattern.

The Rituals

The main kind of ritual usually performed during any of these festivals is the blessing. This is a word derived from the Old English *bletsian,* which meant to perform sacrifice, or really more literally to besprinkle with blood. Only later was it Christianized, like so much else in the religious terminology of the ancient Troth. The Icelandic or Old Norse term for this is *blót,* and it is often used to refer to this kind of rite as well.

There has been a good deal of misunderstanding about the concept of "sacrifice" in recent years. The word is not of Germanic origin, but is derived from the Latin. Even there, however, it means simply "to make sacrosanct or holy." Our idea that to sacrifice something is to throw it away in a superstitious folly comes from the observation of Middle Eastern sacrificial practices—such as those you can read about in the Old Testament. In the Germanic world this kind of activity was unknown. Animals were "sacrificed," but the word used means really nothing more than "given," to the Gods and Goddesses. When we give something, a birthday gift to a friend, for example, we strengthen the bonds of friendship and fellowship with that person. When the ancient Teutons gave something to the Gods they were likewise strengthening their bonds of fellowship and even kinship with the Gods and Goddesses. After all. our ancestors knew themselves to be literally descended from the Gods themselves. The blessings are times when we can enjoy the fellowship of the Gods. Animal sacrifice is no longer practiced in the Troth.

The basic equipment for carrying out Troth-blessings consists of an altar, which can be of stone or wood; a drinking vessel (preferably a drinking horn); a bowl; and a sprig of evergreen. The rites are usually performed outdoors. If they are held indoors the altar is usually made of wood and is called a stall, and if outdoors the altar is usually made of stone and called a harrow.

The basic ritual formula of the blessing, which can be adapted to any sacred purpose and done to honor or worship any God or Goddess, is as follows:

1. *Hallowing:* This sets the ritual time/space apart from the ordinary. This is done most simply by tracing the sign of the hammer: ⊥ in the four cardinal points. If you have a permanently hallowed stead, or *ve,* there is really no need for this to be hallowed every time you work there.

2. *Reading:* This places the rite in a mythic context; mythic poems or epics are read or recited.

3. *Rede:* This part links the mythic pattern to the purpose of the ritual at hand. This is a simple or elaborate statement of the main purposes of the rite.

4. *Call:* This invokes the deities or classes of beings to be honored in the rite. It is an invitation for these beings to join in the fellowship of humans loyal to them.

5. *Loading:* This "charges" the sacred drink with godly power. This is done by pouring the drink, sometimes mead (honey wine), ale, beer, or fruit juices, into the drinking vessel, and visualizing the collected powers entering into the liquid.

6. *Drinking:* This is the consuming of the

charged liquid and internal circulation of its power. This is done by drinking from the horn by all present. The horn is never drained; something is always left which is poured into the blessing bowl on the altar.

7. *Blessing*: This is the sprinkling of the altar with the sacred liquid. This is done from the sacrificial bowl with a sprig of evergreen by dipping it in the liquid and sprinkling it around the altar.

8. *Giving:* This is the returning of the rightful part of the gathered power back to the divinity and/or to nature. This is done by pouring the contents of the blessing-bowl onto the bare earth.

9. *Leaving:* This is the declaration of the end of the work and of the return to the everyday space/time.

This kind of rite can be performed at all of the important times of the year, in honor of all of the Gods and Goddesses. For a complete system of the religion of the Troth, see my *Book of Troth*.

Beyond the purely "religious" usage of the blessing formula, it can also be used for more directly magical purposes. Again, the line between these two real kinds of activity are often blurred. To use the blessing formula in a magical way, the *vitki* makes a blessing to a specific God or Goddess whose aspect yields a return gift in harmony with the will or desire of the *vitki*. This will or desire is spelled out in some detail in the rede section of the blessing formula. This is not a "prayer," but rather an entering into a mutual contract with the God or Goddess. The divinities want to help their fellow sentient beings—but we must know how to enter into contracts with them, how to interact with them.

As an example of what a true working would look like, I present the full ritual text of the Midsummer Blessing as practiced by the Ring of Troth.

The Midsummer Blessing
(June 21)

This rite should be performed outdoors at noon either on or before the day of the summer solstice.

1. HALLOWING
Beginning in the north, trace the sign of the hammer of Thunar in the air in front of you and say: "Hammer of Thunar hallow this stead!" Turning to the right, do this for all four cardinal directions: east, south and west. Then return to facing the north and say:

This stead is hallowed for our work here today. As the God Heimdall wards the Bifrost Bridge, so this stead is warded against all unholy wights and ways.

2. READING
The lay of "Baldur's Dreams" is read or recited. The text of this can be found in the *Poetic Edda*.

3. REDE
The speaker says:

This noontide of the midsummer we gather together as in days of yore to greet the sun at her highest stead, and to honor all the Gods and Goddesses who dwell in Ásgardhr. We call upon them to make ripe their might and main in our lives. We call upon them all—the holy many—living as a whole as is Woden's law.

4. CALL

The speaker makes the following calls. After each call, if there are any other people present, they should give welcome to the God or Goddess being called with their name, and add the words: *"We give thee welcome!"* For example, after the first line below, the others present would say: *"Woden, we give thee welcome!"*

Woden, we are awed by thy craft,
Tiw, we stay true to thee forever,
Baldur, thy brightness and boldness guide us,
Frigga, thy fruit and wisdom keep us all,
Idunna, thine apples ward our ways,
Thunar, thy thunder wards our stead,
Freia, we get freedom from thy frolic,
Frei, from thee we get a harvest of frith.

Then a list of divine attributes of the Gods and Goddesses just called is recited by the speaker. After each, if there are others present, they should say: *"We give thee welcome!"*

Rune-Lord,
One-Handed God,
Holder of the Hringhorn,

Lady of the Gods and Goddesses,
Keeper of the Apples,
Guardian of Ásgardhr,
Holder of the Brisingamen,
God of the Wane.
Again we call to you in all your names. Be among
us here this noontide as the year reaches its height
and Sunna stands at her strongest stead.

Hail, all the Gods,   hail, all the Goddesses
hail, all holy ones
who dwell all together!

5. LOADING

The speaker pours mead (or some other suitable drink such as apple juice) into the drinking
horn or cup, holds it up high, and says:

We give to you the gifts of our works blended
and woven with the might and main of this mead.
It lends us—Gods and folk together—help in our
striving toward the shining plain where the
worlds and wights dwell in wholeness. The year
has come to its peak of power—the eagle gazes
from the topmost branch of the world-tree—may
his sight find us not wanting in wisdom.

6. DRINKING

The speaker then drinks from the drinking
vessel and pours the remainder into the blessing
bowl on the altar (harrow). The drinking vessel is
then refilled and passed to each of the other persons present. Each makes the sign of the hammer
(⊥) over the rim of the vessel before drinking. The
left over drink is poured into the blessing bowl.

7. BLESSING

The speaker now takes the sprig of evergreen and dips it in the blessing bowl and then sprinkles the altar and any persons who are true to the Gods and Goddesses. While doing this he or she repeats:

The blessings of all the Gods and all the Goddesses of our folk be upon us.

8. GIVING

After the blessing is completed, the speaker pours the contents of the blessing bowl out upon the bare earth to the east of the altar while saying:

To Woden, Tiw, Baldur, Frigga, Idunna, Thunar, Freia, and Frei—and to all the Gods and Goddesses of our folk: for good harvest and frith.

9. LEAVING

The speaker returns to the altar, facing north, and says:

Thus the work is once again wrought. It renews our hearts to do worthy deeds, and to strive toward our goals with mighty moods, wise words, and trust in our own powers—ever holding our oaths to ourselves and to our folk!

7 Runes and Rune-Galdor of the Viking Age

"From the fury of the Northmen, O Lord, deliver us!" This is what a monastic chronicler once wrote when confronted with the onslaught of Viking raids. In Scandinavia the time between 800 and 1100 C.E. is known as the Viking Age. This was a time of great cultural vigor in the North. It was the age when the mysteries of the 16 runes of the younger runic futhark were the established way the true Northern magicians encoded their secrets.

Not everybody living in Scandinavia or its colonies during the so-called Viking Age was actually a **Viking**. "Viking" is a description of an activity and persons who engage in that activity, not of the whole culture. To become a Viking meant making trips over the world outside Scandinavia for purposes of trading and raiding (pirating). For the most part those who took part in the Viking activities were noblemen, free landholders, and freemen. As such there was certainly a

great number among them who were knowledgeable about runes and their mysteries.

Until now, virtually nothing has been written about the 16-rune futhark from an esoteric
point of view. This has been unfortunate. For
while pseudo-runic systems were being spewed
out, true runic traditions were still lying hidden
waiting to be brought forth from the dark edges
and corners of the past. Here I will, for the first
time, discuss the purely esoteric aspects of the
younger futhark in its own right—the true mystery tradition of the Vikings.

An advantage to working with the 16-rune
futhark is that the great bulk of written records are
in Icelandic—the language historically in harmony
with and suited to the younger futhark system. For
this reason written Icelandic documents can easily
be "runicized"; that is, transliterated into runic
characters. The advantages of this for purposes of
magic and rune-wisdom are very great indeed.

The Word Rune

To understand the runic system of magic, no
matter which system it is you are working with,
you must know what the word "rune" really
means. One secret tradition holds that "rune," or
a formula containing that word, is what the Galdor Father (Ódhinn) whispered into the ear of his
dead son, Baldur, as he lay on his funeral bier.
This word, whispered "through Baldur's ear," now
echoes throughout the ages—and has been heard
and acted upon by present day Erulians, or Runemasters.

Interestingly enough the word "rune" (Ice. *rún*) does not mean "letter" or "character" but rather a "secret" or "mystery." It is the equivalent of the Latin *arcanum* (as in the terminology of the Tarot) or the Greek *mysterion*, mystery. This gives the most important clue to the word's true meaning. Systems of **runes** are not first and foremost systems of "letters" in the profane sense, but rather systems of secrets or mysteries. All of the individual secrets are ultimately derived from a primordial great secret or mystery—the **Rune**. Originally the word comes from an ancient root meaning to whisper or roar, and to inquire or ask. Thus we see that the word has two different edges—an active one which can cause changes to occur through the power of the voice and one which exhorts to an eternal quest, a seeking of answers even to seemingly imponderable questions.

Leading the way to understanding the word is its basic meaning of mystery. It is the **hidden**, that which lies just beyond our mental and spiritual grasp. This sense of the hidden or mysterious in our lives is what pulls us ever onward to new adventures, new frontiers, and new discoveries. Without this intuitive sense that there is more to reality than what we sense with our five senses in the realm of three dimensions, there could be no progress, no evolution in consciousness. This universal mystery was comprehended by the ancient Teutons and intuitively systematized and culturally encoded in the runic tradition.

Regardless of whether you are a beginner in the field of esoteric studies or an advanced initiate, on some level you can easily understand the

concept embedded in the original concept of the
"Runic"—the occult. The Odian branch of the
Northern way is a tradition based on the concept
encoded in this word. As such it is perhaps the
system of magic best suited to a continuously
active or dynamic search or quest for an eternally
elusive goal. *The power of the Rune lies in its ability to spur seekers onward.* Because no *end* is
thirsted for, the seeker on the Northern path
measures success in progress made. Success is
gauged by the ground you cover, not the goals
met. At his level the Rune is a universal principle,
more or less comprehensible in all systems of
magic or religion. However, it is only the Odian
tradition which has focused on this as an object or
aim in and of itself.

Underlying the whole of the runic systems as
we know them historically is the overriding concept of the Rune. But within the magical runic traditions there are many avenues and roadways by
which to approach these universal mysteries. It is
clear that a **rune** is not simply a letter or character
in an alphabet—it is that and much more. Every
rune is made up of three elements or aspects:

1) a sound (song)
2) a stave (shape)
3) a rune (hidden lore)

No one part of this triad can stand totally
alone—each implies and projects the other. The
sound or phonetic value of the rune is its vibratory
quality in the air, in space. This is the magical-
creative quality that is inherent in speech. It is

this quality we think of when we hear about "the word of God," or the *Logos* (Word), the creative *vac* of Brahma, and so on. This is a cosmic principle with which runesters work when they sing or speak the runes in acts of galdor. The shape of the rune-stave is the spatial or visible quality of the rune. This aspect can be the most deceptive because we put so much emphasis on what we see. The visible staves (characters) are only reflections of the actual runes, which remain forever hidden from our five senses. They exist in a realm beyond the three dimensions and are only approximated in the two-dimensional diagrams we can see. The runes themselves are complex and multifaceted and fit within a web-work which only further complicates the picture. No one definition of a rune is possible, for each rune is in and of itself infinite and without bounds. In practical terms the rune is the sum total of lore and information on the stave and the sound. The song is the vibration, the stave is the image, and the rune is the lore needed to activate the magic.

All true runic traditions take certain factors into careful account. These are: the order of the staves (this gives their numerical value) and their total number (16, 24), a threefold division of the total number (into *ættir*), the shapes of individual staves, their sounds or phonetic values, their special rune-names, and a body of complex poetic lore surrounding each stave. Each of these elements has its esoteric reason for being there. If the runes were merely a system for writing, all that would be needed would be the visible sign and a conventionally agreed on sound value.

The runic system has its origins in the dim past. No one really knows where or when the system of rune-staves was first used. The best guess is that it was sometime before 200 B.C.E. The oldest known system of runes is the 24-fold or elder futhark.

Lore of the Elder Futhark

Name	Sound	Shape	Meaning
fehu	f	ᚠ	CATTLE (wealth, dynamic power)
ūruz	u	ᚢ	AUROCHS (vital formative force)
thurisaz	th	ᚦ	THURS (giant, breaker of resistance)
ansuz	a	ᚨ	GOD (Woden, sovereign ancestral God)
raidho	r	ᚱ	CHARIOT (vehicle on path of power)
kēnaz	k	ᚲ	TORCH (controlled energy)
gebō	g	ᚷ	GIFT (exchanged powers)
wunjō	w	ᚹ	JOY (harmony of like forces)
hagalaz	h	ᚻ	HAIL (destruction, seed form)
nauthiz	n	ᚾ	NEED (distress, self-created fire)
īsa	i	ᛁ	ICE (contraction)
jēra	j (y)	ᛃ	YEAR (good harvest, orbits, cycles)

îhwaz	i	∫	YEW (axis of heaven-earth-hel)
perthrō	p	⌊	LOTBOX (evolutionary force)
elhaz	-z	Y	ELK (protective teaching force)
sowilō	s	⟨	SUN (sun-wheel, crystal-ized light)
tîwaz	t	↑	TYR (sky-god, sovereign order)
berkanō	b	ß	BIRCH (-GODDESS, container/releaser)
ehwaz	e	M	HORSE (trust, coopera-tion)
mannaz	m	M	HUMAN (psychic order of the gods)
laguz	l	Γ	WATER (life energy, organic growth)
ingwaz	ng	◇	ING (earth-god, gestation process)
dagaz	d	M	DAY (twilight/dawn paradox)
ōthala	o	◊	ESTATE (ancestral spiri-tual power)

There was also an Anglo-Frisian futhorc which was an extension of the basic 24-rune elder futhark. The Anglo-Frisian system was in use from as early as 400 to around 1100 C.E., but in Scandinavia the elder futhark evolved into the younger futhark of 16 runes. This system shows the overridingly magical nature of the runes in that, from a purely linguistic standpoint, it made the system more obscure While the language that the writing system was designed to represent was becoming more complex, the system of characters was simplified. The total of runes was reduced from 24 to 16 characters. Beyond this the signs themselves were simplified. This usually involved the reduction of two-staved runes to a single stave.

The Younger Futhark

Name	Sound	Shape	Meaning
fé	f	ᚡ	Livestock, gold, wealth
úr	u/o/v	ᚢ	Drizzle or slag or aurochs
thurs	th/dh	ᚦ	Thurs (giant)
áss	a	ᚬ	God (Odhinn)
reidh	r	ᚱ	Riding or thunderclap
kaun	klg/ng	ᚴ	A sore
hagall	h	ᚼ	Hail
naudh	n	ᚾ	Need
íss	i/e/j	ᛁ	Ice
ár	a	ᛅ	Good year/harvest
sól	s	ᛋ	Sun
Týr	t/d/nd	ᛏ	Týr (sky-god)

bjarkan	b/p/mb	ᛒ	Birch(-Goddess)
madhr	m	ᛘ	Man (human being)
lögr	l	ᛚ	Water or sea or waterfall
ýr	-r	ᛦ	Yew or yew bow

A more detailed table for turning Icelandic or Old Norse words into their runic versions is given in Appendix A.

It cannot be overemphasized that this reformation of the runic system really reflects a reformation in the ancient rune-gild order. The system became "leaner and meaner" in the Viking Age, but it authentically retained the lore and mysteries of the elder futhark in more condensed form.

In the tables on the following pages I will present the lore of the true Viking runes—the ones actually used in the Viking Age. This material has never before been presented in this way. There is a vast storehouse of wisdom and magical power available in the runes of the younger futhark because it is the system that preserves so much of the myth and lore of the ancient North.

Among the most important aspects of the lore are the rune poems. The runic stanzas of these poems are given in the tables. The first stanza is from the "Old Norwegian Rune Rhyme," and the second is from the "Old Icelandic Rune Poem." These poems were composed from within the younger runic tradition, and so they are truly and completely authentic to the system being explained. The original language follows the

English translation immediately. The originals will be found to be of great value in creating practical magical talismans and so forth. On the tape *Rune Song* you can hear the sound of the original language of the poems.

For magical or divinatory purposes, there is no higher authority than the rune poems coupled with your knowledge of the lore and your own intuition.

fé
(Wealth)

(Gold) causes strife among kinsmen;
the wolf grows up in the woods.

*(Fé) veldr frænda rógi;
fœðisk úlfr í skógi.*

(Gold) is the strife of kinsmen,
and fire of the flood-tide,
and the path of the serpent.

*(Fé) er frænda róg
ok flæðar viti
ok grafseiðs gata*

Fé is the rune of mobile power in the world
and in the self. It flows outward like fire. It is a
power which, like money, must be circulated in
order for it to have its beneficial effects. This is
the fire of life and of the movement behind all
continual change in the universe. It is the electro-
magnetic force flowing along the surface of the
earth—"the path of the serpent."

In rune-galdor this rune is beneficial for

works intended to draw wealth or riches. It is also a great source of vital energy. It is a rune by which other rune forces can be projected or sent out.

In divination *fé* indicates that wealth may be involved. But at the same time there may be conflicts brought about because of it. There will be new beginnings in life. Negative aspects of the rune include a tendency toward greed. If the power of *fé* is not given and received freely—with generosity—it will begin to destroy a person.

2

ur
(Drizzle)

(Slag) is from bad iron;
   oft runs the reindeer on the hard snow.

*(Úr) es af illu járni;
   opt hleypr hreinn á hjarni.*

(Drizzle) is the weeping of clouds,
   and the lessener of the rim of ice,
   and what the herdsman hates.

*(Úr) er skyja gratr
   ok skara þverir
   ok hirðis hatr.*

In the elder futhark *uruz* means aurochs or
urus—a now-extinct European bison. But because
this rune-stave took on so many other meanings
as a result of the runic reform around 800 C.E.,
the meaning was also slightly changed. The
U-rune now accommodated the mysteries of the
w-stave *(wunjö)* and the o-stave *(öthala)*. *Úr* is the
vital organic energy of life and the power which
organizes and holds life together. It is a power of

purification. *Úr* drives out elements that may cause one to be weak. This is a purification that leads to strength.

In galdor the power of *Úr* can be used to bind other runes together in an organized fashion. It is a sign of tenacious will power. This rune is beneficial in workings of healing and regeneration of the body.

In runecasting it is a sign of a striving toward inner goals or those which will serve one's fellows. The subject is willful and tenacious. There is a striving toward freedom and independence. If poorly aspected, the rune may imply weakness, obsession, or domination by others.

thurs
("Giant")

(Thurs) causes the woe of women;
few are cheerful from misfortune.

(Þurs) veldr kvenna kvillu;
kátr verðr fár af illu.

(Thurs) is the woe of women,
and a dweller in the rocks,
and the husband of the etin-wife
Vardh-runa.

(Þurs) er kvenna kvöl
ok kletta búi
ok varðrúnar verr.

A *thurs* is a force in nature. It is a force
which reacts to consciousness in a negative way.
It is the force of opposition in the world. The
thurses (giants) are preconscious, pre-divine
beings which are the natural opponents of the
Æsir and Vanir. The force which they embody is
wielded against them by the God Ása-Thórr—in a
sort of cosmic homeopathy. Thorr fights fire with

fire, ice with ice.

For magical purposes the *thurs*, if it can be "tamed," is a powerful form of aggressive defense. It is analogous to the "Hammer of Thórr." The th-stave can also be used to combine two opposing or polarized forces into a kinetic form of energy. This can also be used in sex-magical rites—but it must be used with caution.

In divinatory readings the th-stave may show that you are being opposed by outside forces—perhaps forces unknown to you at this time. A crisis is forthcoming; it may act as a catalyst for change. Use it wisely. Betrayal may be in the involved.

4

áss
(God)

(Estuary) is the way of most journeys,
    but the sheath is such for swords.

(Óss) es flestra ferða för;
    en skálpr es sverða.

(Ase) is the olden-father,
    and Asgardhr's chieftain,
        and the leader of Valhalla.

(Áss) er aldingautr
    ok ásgarðs jöfurr,
        ok valhallar vísi.

This is the rune of Ódhinn—the Galdor-Father. Ódhinn is the ancestral model of divine and sovereign consciousness in humanity. This is the God of transformation. The very form (or archetype) of Ódhinn serves as a pattern, a model example, for those who call themselves Odians. The reference to the "estuary" in the "Old Norwegian Rune Rhyme" is interesting in light of C. G. Jung's comparison of archetypes to riverbeds (see

p. 40). The riverbeds are the patterns of consciousness; what is needed is the life-force to revive them.

You will note that in the younger futhark there are really two a-runes (ᛆ and ᛅ). This again points to the magical rather than linguistic reasons behind the runic reform from the 24-rune system to the 16-rune row. The *áss*-rune is only rarely used. (See Appendix A on the transliteration of runes.)

In galdor the a-stave is the sign of god-like consciousness and wisdom. It is also the rune of ecstasy and poetic inspiration. Use this rune to invoke these powers—and to master the power of the word.

For rune-cast readings the a-stave discloses that some kind of inspiration or knowledge is present. Answers are to be sought in inspiration and intuition, combined in equal parts with intellectual and rational inquiry. This is the essence of the runic method. If the rune seems negative or reversed, it could mean delusion and misunderstanding.

reidh
(Riding)

(Riding), it is said, is the worst for horses;
   Reginn forged the best sword.

(Reið) kveða hrossum versta;
   Reginn sló sverðit bezta.

(Riding) is a blessed sitting,
   and a swift journey,
      and the toil of the horse.

(Reið) er sitjandi sæla
   ok snúðig ferð
      ok jors erfiði.

The *reidh* is the pattern of cyclical, rhythmic, and proportional motion. This is the rune of
the journey of life. The "riding" is also the vehicle
of the initiatory journey. (It can also mean a
"chariot.") This journey is a pathway to power,
but it can be very hard on the body in and on
which the soul (in all its forms) is seen to "ride."

In the practice of magic the r-stave is useful
as a force to guide magical energies along their

right pathways. It is a guide to finding higher counsel (rede). Through it success in legal matters can be obtained.

In divination *reidh* indicates that rationality, justice, and ordered growth are present in the subject's journey through life. Help may come from unexpected sources. The rune may show the influence of an institution of some kind. If the rune is negatively aspected, it may mean crisis, stand-still, and even injustice and irrationality.

kaun
(Sore)

(Sore) is of bairns the bale;
  grief makes a man pale.

(Kaun) es beygja barna;
  böl gørir mann fölvan.

(Sore) is the bale of bairns,
  and a scourge,
    and a house of foul flesh.

(Kaun) er barna böl
  ok bardaga för
  ok holdfúa hús.

Kaun is the power of fire to break things up
into their component parts—to analyze them.
Uncontrolled, this can be destructive (as empha-
sized in the stanzas of the rune poems). It is
indeed a difficult power to master and control.
But if it is controlled it becomes the principle of
creativity—the controlled fire of the pyre, forge,
hearth, and harrow.

The k-stave has also taken on the symbolic

qualities of the g-rune and the ng-rune. As such the *kaun* is also a symbol of generosity and exchange and hospitality. It is the rune of procreation, of gestation, and of coming to fruition.

In the work of galdor the k-stave is useful in magic aimed at controlling energy, toward creative purposes, and in acts of sex magic of all kinds.

For divinatory purposes *kaun* first points to the tendency toward degeneration, disease, or decay. If it is very well aspected it implies that ability, creativity, transformation, and even regeneration are present. Often degeneration must take place before regeneration can. The k-stave counsels rest and relaxation—which will give rise to new inner creativity and inspiration. The power must gestate.

hagall
(Hail)

(Hail) is the coldest of grains;
   Christ shaped the world in olden times.

(Hagall) es kaldastr korna;
   Kristr skóp heim inn forna.

(Hail) is a cold grain,
   and a shower of sleet,
      and the sickness of snakes.

(Hagall) er kaldakorn
   ok krapadrífa
      ok snáka sótt.

The hailstone is a dangerous projectile from the heavens. It can destroy crops—destroy the seeds which have been planted. The h-stave is a rune of crisis and possible misfortune. But it is also the *ice seed* (grain). This is the cosmic seed of the beginning of all things. It is the cosmos in seed form.

For magical purposes the h-stave is most powerful in workings designed for realization of the structure and dynamics of the cosmos (world). It is the seed of knowledge. But it is also effective on a lower level as a powerful weapon or tool for protection.

In rune-casting the *hagall* expresses trauma or crisis on the first level. Change is indicated. If basic "seed" concepts are listened to, and acted upon, a good outcome can perhaps be expected. The present situation must be changed—based on higher principles.

naudh
(Need)

(Need) makes for a difficult plight;
the naked freeze in the frost.

(Nauð) gørir hneppa kosti;
nøktan kelr í frosti.

(Need) is the pain of the bondmaid,
and a hard plight,
and toilsome work.

(Nauð) er þýjar þrá   ok þungr kostr
ok vássamlig verk.

The n-stave reflects the principle of resistance or friction in the world. This is to be understood on all levels of being—in nature, in society, and in the psyche. Although the source of this resistance may be outside the control of the individual, the way in which this resistance or stress can be **used** by the individual is completely within the control of that person. *Naudh* refers to the "need-fire," the kind of fire which is made by friction (with a fire-bore). This is a **self-gener-**

ated fire. To overcome the resistance in *naudh* the energy must come from deep within the self.

Magically, *naudh* is very useful. It can be employed as a psychological tool to overcome distress (or just plain **stress)** in life. Through its power inspiration can be gained and insight into the process of destiny gained. In the course of self-development it is the mystery which points the way to knowledge of one's personal direction or destiny. It is a tool for the development of the personal will.

In divination the n-stave points to friction or opposition. This opposition or resistance is most likely coming **from within.** The situation calls for innovation and original (self-generated) solutions: "Necessity is the mother of invention." It is important to come to recognize your own wyrd.

iss
(Ice)

(Ice), we call the broad bridge;
   the blind need to be led.

(Íss) köllum brú breiða;
   blindan þarf at leiða.

(Ice) is the rind of the river,
   and the roof of the waves,
      and a danger for dying men.

(Íss) er árbörkr
   ok unnar þak
      ok feigra manna fár.

"Ice" in the cosmos is the principle of con-
traction which emanates from Niflheimr. It gath-
ers everything into itself and tries to hold it in
stillness and chill. This force balances the cosmic
fire emanating from Muspellsheimr. The force of
"ice" is a solidifying factor in all things. It is the
gravitational force holding things in place in the
world. This, of course, can be destructive or beneficial. It may be needed to balanced unchecked

motion and chaotic dynamism. But if it is just that movement that is needed, it can be destructive by its imposition of entropy on the situation. The i-stave consolidates and solidifies the ego-consciousness.

In galdor the i-stave is a powerful force for concentrating the will. It can be used as a way to focus ego awareness. But "ice" is also a way to constrain or constrict those elements you wish to "freeze"—to bring to a standstill.

In rune-casting the i-stave indicates a concentration within the self or ego and enforces the idea of unity or focus on a single point in life. This may be detrimental or lead to some kind of egomania or even dull stupidity. There is often a certain degree of stagnation in situations where the i-stave arises.

ar
(Good-Year)

(Harvest) is the profit of men;
   I say that Frodhi was generous.

(Ár) es gumna góði;
   getk at örr vas Fróði.

(Harvest) is the profit of all men,
   and a good summer,
      and a ripened field.

(Ár) er gumna góði
   ok gott sumar
      ok algróinn akr.

This is the rune of the eternal return according to the cycles of nature and also those in the
metaphysical realm. It is in and of itself a great
good. At Midsummer during the Viking Age the
Northern folk gave gifts to the Gods and Goddesses *til árs ok fridhar* (for good harvest *[ár]* and
peace *[frith]*). The a-rune implies both great prosperity and the peace such will bring. Frodhi is a
mythical king of Denmark who made the land

very prosperous and thereby brought "the peace of Frodhi" to the land.

Historically the a-stave developed from the old *jēra*-rune and thus has taken on many of its esoteric qualities as well.

In magic the *ár*-rune is a sign used to invoke the power of harmonious enlightenment. It promotes higher knowledge and realization of the cycles of the world. It is a sign of the runes (mysteries) being brought into manifestation in the world.

The a-stave is the rune of reward for the actions of the past. The subject of the rune-cast receives peace and tranquility—if that is the just reward. Cycles of nature are come full circle in the a-stave. There is plenty and peace in life. If the rune is in a bad aspect, or if you read the runes in inverse position, the *ár*-rune can mean poverty and conflict.

sól
(Sun)

(Sun) is the light of the lands;
I bow down to the doom of holiness.

*(Sól) es landa ljómi;
lútik helgum dómi.*

(Sun) is the shield of the clouds,
and shining glory,
and the life-long sorrow of ice.

*(Sól) er skyja skjöldr
ok skínandi röðull
ok ísa aldrtregi.*

The sun is the bringer of organic life and its
sustainer. The sun is a nurturing force in the
North. Perhaps this is why the sun is seen as
being essentially **feminine** in Germanic mythology. Sunna is the Norse Goddess of the Sun. The
sun banishes and gently and persistently destroys
the forces of restriction and constraint—in the
form of ice *(íss)*. This is a sign according to which
initiatory journeys are oriented—it is by the light

of *sól* that spiritual navigators steer their courses.

Magically *sól* is most beneficial as a guiding beacon to higher goals of consciousness. It can also protect the magician and give success in navigating the rough seas of life. It is the power by which the magician can break through the barriers to higher being.

In divinatory readings the s-stave offers guidance and hope. It promises success. But it also counsels you to set your goals and remain true to them. The s-stave can be a powerful sign of the breakthrough of higher powers from beyond one's present life. Its only negative aspect is that you may be deluded into thinking you have been successful, or that you have goals, when in fact you have not made contact with your higher counsel. Seek the sun.

tyr
(Týr)

(Týr) is the one-handed among the Æsir;
   the smith has to blow often.

(Týr) es einhendr Ása;
   opt verðr smiðr at blása.

(Týr) is the one-handed god,
   and the left-overs of the wolf,
      and the ruler of the temple.

(Týr) er einnendr áss
   ok úlfs leifar
      ok hofa hilmir.

In the Viking Age tradition the *týr*-rune refers quite directly to the God Týr (English Tiw). Týr is the God of law and order in the cosmos. His original work in the shaping of the universe was to open up space in the cosmos in which further creation (shaping) might take place. But beyond this, Týr is the God of Self-Sacrifice. Both of the rune poems refer to the myth in which Týr lost a hand to the Fenris Wolf, who was causing havoc in Ásgardhr. Because the Gods did not want to shed the blood of the Wolf, they bound him with a magical cord. But before the Wolf would allow the Gods to put the cord around him, he demanded that Týr put his hand in his maw as a pledge of good faith. When the fetter held the Wolf, he snapped Týr's hand off at the wrist (which is called the wolf's joint).

Galdor-work that can be done through the power of the t-stave includes obtaining success or justice (the t-rune is the rune of victory). It is also the sign of knowledge gained through Ódhinn's self-sacrifice. It is the rune by which the unity of opposites is realized.

In divination the *týr*-rune points to the presence of loyalty and faithfulness in your life. It is the power of the purest form of justice. There may be some sacrifice of your own self-interest involved. You are counselled to analyze the situation—apply rational thought to any problem and act on the conclusions. Logic is called for. At the same time, if this rune is badly aspected or reversed, it could imply a tendency to over-analysis or the presence of injustice in your life.

bjarkan
(Birch-twig)

(Birch-twig) is the limb greenest with leaves;
Loki brought the luck of deceit.

(Bjarkan)'s laufgrœnstr líma;
Loki bar flæðar tíma.

(Birch-twig) is a leafy limb,
    and a little tree,
        and a youthful wood.

(Bjarkan) er laufgat lim
    ok lítit tré
        ok ungsamligr viðr.

This rune name originally refers not the
birch tree as such, for which the Icelandic word is
simply *björk,* but rather to the Birch-Goddess—
Freyja. This is the rune of transformation and
becoming. The b-stave rules the process of birth-
life-death-rebirth in nature and beyond.

The b-stave has taken in the older meanings
of the p-stave *(perthro),* as well as having taken
over its sound value. It is the stave of becoming in

a realm beyond the bounds of nature. It is the rune of the mysteries of *wyrd*. Wyrd (or weird) is the result of our past actions (perhaps from previous "life-times"). These remain hidden to the non-initiate. The b-stave is a sign of these "hidden" influences and is the introspective path to uncovering them.

In magic the b-stave is the rune of concealment and protection. It is the shelter in which transformation can take place. The b-stave describes the process of creative evolution. It brings all processes to their fruitful conclusions in manifestation.

Bjarkan is the stave of new beginnings and transformations based on eternal patterns. There is gradual and natural change. Spiritual growth takes place within a traditional framework. There is a growth in the subject's understanding of the process of wyrd ("fate"). If badly placed, the b-stave can show a blurring of awareness or stagnation in growth.

madhr
(Man)

(Man) is the increase of dust;
   mighty is the talon-span of the hawk.

(Maðr) es moldar auki,
   mikil es grelp á hauki.

(Man) is the joy of man,
   and the increase of dust,
      and the adornment of ships.

(Maðr) er manns gaman   ok moldar auki
   ok skipa skreytir.

This is the rune of humanity. The most
ancient name of this rune, *mannaz,* essentially
means mankind, not just "man." The m-stave is the
symbol of the mystery of humanity—the only other
kind of being in the cosmos sharing the spiritual
gifts of the divine archetypes of consciousness.

Humans are born mortal. This ensures their
opportunity to transform themselves. Mortality is
also a unique gift of the Gods of Consciousness.
This is why there is an emphasis on mortality in

the rune poems—*madhr er moldar auki* (man is the increase of dust) is repeated in both poems.

The m-stave is a model of the divine structure present in the psychic make up of humans and the reflection of that structure in the social, political, and religious models humans shape and reshape for themselves.

Magically *madhr* is the rune which unlocks the storehouse of imagery stored in the mind's hidden eye. The m-stave is a sign which promotes deep knowledge, wisdom, and intelligence. It can be used as a symbol for dynamic balancing of the personality.

The m-stave in rune-casting means that the divine structure of consciousness and of the Gods and Goddesses is present. Intelligence and awareness are called for and are to be found in the situation. The m-stave counsels a clear and deep assessment of the subject's position in life. Danger may lie in depression or self-delusion if the stave is badly aspected.

lögr
(Water)

(Water) is what falls from the mountain
  `tis a force; but gold tokens are costly
    things.

(Lögr)'s es fellr ór fjalli, foss;
  en gull eru hnossir.

(Water) is a churning lake,
  and a wide kettle,
    and the land of fish.

(Lögr) er vellanda vatn
  ok víðr ketill
    ok glommunga grund.

This is the primeval cosmic water welling up
from the depths of Niflheimr. The l-stave is the
sign of the waters of life. It is the rune of organic
life itself and of the pathway to and from that
state of being. It is through water we come into
the world, and it is over water we must journey
on our return to the well-spring of life, or to the
realm of Valhalla. In the mythology of the North

there is a whole cosmological structure of mythical rivers and streams of water over and along which the initiate, shaman, or dead man must pass in order to reach a destination.

In the sphere of magical workings the I-stave is most effective as a tool for increasing one's intuition and for developing one's force of vital power. It can also be used as a support through the tough tests which life throws up before us.

The I-stave may indicate that stern tests lie ahead, but that the power and force of vital organic life is present. The realm of the unconscious is near. There is growth and chance in the offing. If the rune is badly aspected it can imply that the life force is diminishing or that the subject of the reading is being victimized by anxiety or fears—perhaps irrational ones.

yr
(Yew)

(Yew) is the greenest wood in winter;
   there is oft singeing when it burns.

(Yr) es vetrgrœstr viða;
   vant's, es brennr, at svíða

(Yew) is a strung bow,
   and brittle iron,
      and a giant of the arrow.

(Yr) er bendr bogi
   ok brotgjarnt járn
      ok fífu fárbauti.

This is the cosmic span between the infinite
world above and the infinite world below—
between Asgardhr and Midhgardhr—between life
and death. The *yr*-rune is full of tension, of potential energy just waiting to be released. This is like
the energy contained in the bowstring, or in wood
before it is burned, or iron before it is tempered.

The yew is the tree of eternal life—it may
live to be more than 2000 years old. It is also the

tree of death, because its needles and berries are poisonous. The kind of toxin carried by the yew cannot cause "intoxication"—only death. The power of the yew-rune is something that should be approached only with great caution and respect. Do not use its power frivolously.

Because the wood is so hard and flexible, it was the favored material for making wooden bows in ancient times. It was also a favorite material for making runic amulets and talismans.

In the runic reform the yew-rune was moved from its 13th position to the end of the reformed row and its sound value was provided by the old 15th rune *(elhaz)*. The *yr*-rune is thus a combination of the old yew and elk runes.

In galdor-work the *yr*-rune is a powerful sign of both vital life-force and of the compelling forces of death. The yew is a mighty protector, but it is also the basis of the most powerful death curses. Through the sign of the *yr*-rune contact with praeternatural entities is possible. It is also one of the most powerful symbols to be used for attracting a lover or partner for erotic magic.

In rune-readings, the *yr*-rune indicates the termination or conclusion of a process. It may also point to a sense of eternity or timelessness which arises from its qualities of endurance. There may be enlightenment at the end of the process. Its power may exert a protective influence over the life of the subject. If badly aspected, the *yr*-rune may imply a poor outcome for the question or one fraught with continued confusion. A magical solution is needed.

Rune-Work

To really prepare for working effective rune galdor or magic, you as an aspiring *vitki* must spend a good deal of time and effort at **making the runes your own.** By this I mean that, although the runes have a definite transpersonal value and reality, these realities have to be discovered and activated **from within** the runester in order to be useful for magical work.

The process of activating the runes within yourself takes some time, but the magical benefits to be derived from it are almost without limit. The training curriculum contained in *The Nine Doors of Midgard* is a complete course in this method. But the practical *vitki* need not spend as much time and effort as that course requires before being able to gain practical results.

RUNE THINKING

You must first really **hear** and **understand** the runes—deep down in the depths of your being —before you can begin to use them magically.

Note that the following exercises are designed for use with the younger futhark of 16 runes. You may, if you wish, use the elder futhark of 24 runes. The system of the elder futhark has been amply outlined in my previous works.

Begin with the first rune, *fé,* and spend one to nine days on each rune. Keep working on each rune until you are satisfied that it has "clicked into place" for you. Meditate on it, visualize it, draw it, sing its name, recite and learn its poetic stanzas. Do anything and everything you can think of to cause your whole mind to absorb the value and meaning, the shape and sound of the runestave.

These exercises can be done in a formal, ritualistic way, or they can just be impromptu sessions. The important thing is to **learn** the rune at a deep level. In this process there is conscious learning going on, but there is also a great deal of unconscious absorption of subtle elements that the rune is transmitting to you directly. These elements will perhaps only come out later in rune-casts or in acts of rune galdor.

In doing this work you should create a schedule for yourself, write it down, and keep a diary of your results, thoughts, and realizations in the process. These notes will be of great practical value later.

During this process you may be doing other magical experiments with or without runes, but just keep up your steady work of absorbing the lore of the 16 or 24 runes as you go.

RUNE RISTING

Once you have taken in the lore of the runes, you are more ready than ever to put this deeply ingrained information into magical practice.

As an initial and systematic act of active rune magic it might be best if you risted (carved) a complete set of rune-lots or rune-tines. These can be used for divinatory purposes later.

Rist one rune per day into a different stick of wood and color it if you wish. One rune is carved per stick. As much as possible you should follow the ritual procedures outlined later in this chap-

ter. Then these single staves will be true talismans—true *taufr*. At the end of the cycle of rune-
ristings you will have a set of powerful talismanic
runestaves, and you will have learned the very
basics of rune-risting.

This is an excellent first exercise in active
rune magic because you are doing nothing more
than creating runic talismans at the most basic
and simple level. You are guaranteed to be successful because the aim of the workings is simply
to load the runic value into the stave for your
later use. This will happen to some extent just by
carving the rune shape into the wood, but your
will and magical intention will reinforce this
many times over.

The techniques learned here will really
begin to pay off in the creation of runic *taufr* as
explained at the end of this chapter.

Once you have completed a runestave talisman, put it in a special place such as a cloth or
leather bag or in a wooden box used exclusively
for this purpose.

See Appendix B for technical pointers on the
actual carving of runic characters into the wood.

Rune Casting

In rune casting, or runic divination, the *vitki*
is opened up to communication directly between
the runes and his or her hidge and myne—under
the guidance of the wode (inspiration). (See glossary for more on these terms.) In reading a rune-
cast you are actively listening to the messages of
the runestaves as they open up deeper levels of

your understanding as applied to a specific situation or question. In many ways rune-casting is a practical tool for opening the purely analytical mind (hidge) to intuitive levels of knowledge—but to do so in a reliable and objective way—which is in the true spirit of rune galdor.

THE RITUAL OF RUNECASTING

In the process of getting the "feel" for the interpretation of runes in given layouts the runecaster will sometimes want to make "hypothetical readings" which are primarily for learning purposes. These may or may not be highly significant. But when a serious inquiry is being made, it should not be taken lightly. You ought to be able to "ask the runes aright" before you can trust them to give you correct readings. In order to ensure the proper framework for such a reading, you might want to establish a traditional ritual setting. This gives a signal to your inner runic sense so that a strong link can be made between the objective and subjective worlds. In this state rune readings will be more effective and trustworthy.

Some find it ideal to work with another student of runecasting in the learning process. In this situation each may learn a great deal from the other, and a greater sense of objectivity can be gained.

THE WORK OF RUNECASTING

1) Sit at a table with a white cloth or piece of paper in front of you. Spend some time settling your thoughts. You may do some kind of hammer-rite to guard your mind from distractions, if you

wish. When you are ready to begin the layout, end your period of preparation with the words:

World all-wide, I shall read the rune aright!

[This establishes the objective field into which the runes will be laid out and read—or projected and analyzed.]

2) Call upon the three-fold Nornic force with these or similar words:

Wend forth out' the wide worlds
ye maidens all-mighty
out' the eastern darkness enter
—Urdhr—Verdhandi—Skuld—
within you I lay the lots!

3) Holding the runestaves in your hands before you with your head uplifted, silently and intently focus in on the question or situation of concern. You may also sing, silently or aloud, the names: *Urdhr-Verdhandi-Skuld.* Once you feel the link has been made, end this part with the words:

Runes rown right rede!
(or in Icelandic: *Rúnar rádha rétt rádh!*)

[This establishes a bond between the exact form of your question and the gathered processes of the "Nornic forces."]

4) Now, randomly choose the number of staves needed for the kind of layout you are doing

from the bundle in your hands and lay them out in one of the predetermined patterns (see below). You might want to sing the Nornic names—*Urdhr—Verdhandi—Skuld*—as you lay out the runes.

5) You now have the proper layout before you. Spend some time looking at the runes and begin to read them aright. You may take as long to interpret the data as necessary.

6) After interpreting (reading) the runes, make a record of the layout in a notebook prepared for this purpose. Certain significant aspects of readings may not be realized until later on, so it is important to keep records of all castings. Now, silently and solemnly return the staves to their place of storage (in their box or cloth bag) and perform the customary closing working.

7) You may now wish to elaborate on your record of the casting or write a more detailed interpretation. Objectifying the reading in this way can be most valuable. It prevents the tendency for rune-readings to shift about in the subjective universe of the reader and become distorted. You may alter your reading later—based on new insights or increased knowledge—but at least have a definite reading to work from.

THE PRACTICE OF RUNE-READING

There are a great number of methods of rune-casting or rune-laying, all of which basically work on the juxtaposition of the runestaves to predetermined steads or positions in a layout pattern. Each of these positions has a special meaning for the interpretation. The reading is a bringing together of the meanings of the rune and the stead in the mind of the runester.

LAYOUT METHODS

The most basic set of meanings for the positions is based on the special Germanic threefold division of time and is related to the way the three great Norns work in the universe. The basic significances of the three Nornic steads are:

Urdhr: That which has become—the past, that which is, which exists in the objective universe, not subject to change, and at the root of the situation in question.

Verdhandi: That which is becoming—the present, that which is fluctuating, which is existing in the eternal now of the subjective world, not only subject to change but the "stuff" of change itself, and the narrow trunk of the present aspect of the situation in question.

Skuld: That which ought to **(should)** become given the functions of Urdhr and Verdhandi—the "future," that which is yet-is-not, which may be, the branches (or one of them) of the situation in question.

As many may already know, the "theory of time" posited by the Urdhr-Verdhandi-Skuld model or process is not a linear one of:

Past→Present→Future

But rather it is one of dynamic opposition between the vast field of significant (real) past action (Urdhr) and the ever-present point of (real) existence—the synthesis of which will result in predictable channels. The vast field of "pastness" and the ever-present "nowness" are the only two realities—Skuld is a state of potentialities. This model of time accounts for many things in the traditional Germanic ideology; for example, the importance of the past and an emphasis on present action.

As far as rune-casting is concerned, a thorough intuitive understanding of these concepts will be indispensable in making meaningful readings, and the use of this pattern will be seen as the mainstay of most casting methods. This, along with the eightfold division of the heavens, is the best indicator of the relative values of the divinatory steads of ancient rune-casting methods.

Often the term "aspect" is mentioned in talking about rune lots and their reading. A lot may be read as either positive or negative, or one lot may be either positively or negatively aspected or related to another. Determining these aspects will help you read the runes most accurately. One way to determine whether a rune lot is positive or negative is by deciding before you lay them out that, if a rune is either face down or reversed when you lay it down, it is negative. But this method is of modern origin and has little in the tradition to recommend it.

The best way to determine aspect is by referring to the angles of relationship of the runes when they are laid around in the cosmic eightfold map of the universe—the eights. This arrangement is shown in Figure 5.

Runes which are at 45- or 135-degree angle

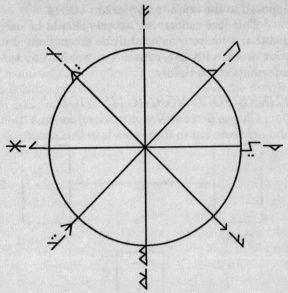

*Figure 5: The Younger Futhark
in the Cosmic Eights*

relationships to one another are positively aspected, while those at a 90-degree or 180-degree relationship are negative. But those at a 180-degree angle will probably have good outcomes ultimately. The 90-degree relationship sets up a blockage of power.

As an example of how this works, look at the *fé*-stave in the figure. Together with the *íss*-stave (to which it can be either positively or negatively aspected), it is positively aspected to the *úr-, ár-, áss-, týr-, kaun-, madhr-, ýr-.* and *naudh*-staves, but it is negatively aspected to the *hagall-, lögr-, thurs-,* and *sól*-staves. It is also negatively opposed to the *reidh-* and *bjarkan*-staves.

This lore concerning aspects should be used together with your own intuition strengthened in your work with the runes. Try not to use this information too rigidly.

THREE-FOLD NORNIC METHOD

Choose three staves at random, one at a time, and lay them out in three steads in this order:

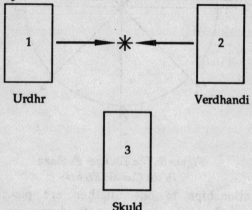

In reading this pattern first turn your attention to Urdhr in her own right—what does she mean in relation to the question? Then turn your thoughts to Verdhandi in a similar fashion. Now relate the Urdhr and Verdhandi steads and see how the Skuld stead represents a coming together of the first two.

With analytical inquiries, that is those in which the rune-caster wishes to illuminate his or her present situation or state of being, steads 1 and 2 are of primary importance. They reveal the "present" (2) and its true background (1)—while (3) will indicate the direction things are about to go. On the other hand, in efforts to predict how things are going to be (and, considering the Teutonic view of time and causality, we can see this could be difficult), the Skuld-stead is primary. Skuld delivers the oracular force, while steads 1 and 2 show the foundations of this tendency. (At the same time, in "predictive" work, steads 1 and 2 show us the areas that might need magical alteration in order to avoid harmful potentialities.)

THE VALKNUTR: A NINEFOLD METHOD

An expansion of the threefold method is to be found in the valknutr layout. Again choose nine lots at random and lay them out in the following steads and order:

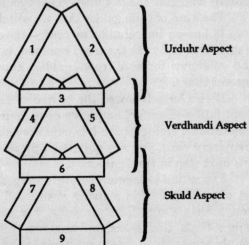

Steads 1-3 represent a detailed picture of the full process of the Urdhr aspect—what is in the background of the situation or question. Steads 4-6 do the same for the Verdhandi aspect—what is happening now with regard to the question—while steads 7-9 show a detailed picture of the process of Skuld as it is yet to unfold.

Because the threefold Nornic process is so fundamental to the craft of rune-casting, the runester should become the master of these two techniques before venturing seriously into other methods.

Rune Galdor

Now the next step is to take the wisdom and knowledge that you have gained up till now in your rune-work and begin to use it more actively in actually changing the circumstances of your life.

The kind of rune galdor that we will discuss here is known in Icelandic as *taufr*—talismanic magic. This is by far the most common, reliable, and effective form of rune galdor known in ancient times.

If you have followed the course of development outlined so far, and have done your runic meditations, created rune-lots, and used them in divinatory rites, you are quite well prepared for this next step in rune galdor.

The actual talismanic creature shaped by an act of rune galdor is a living entity. All living things have their "fate," or *ørlög*. For sentient beings, Gods, Goddesses, and humans, this *ørlög* mainly comes about due to reactions in the objective universe to the actions of that being. Most of these actions have their origins in the inner world of the thinking subject. I must "think" (on some level) of a thing before I do it. In the creation of a talismanic creature, the rune magician shapes a magical being which he or she will endow with a special *ørlög* which it must fulfill. A runic talisman designed to bring one riches will do just that because it is "fated" by the powerful magician to do that and only that. A more elaborate form of *taufr* working which takes this aspect of the rite more into account is presented in *The Nine Doors of Midgard.*

The equipment needed to perform this kind of working includes a knife or other sharp instrument (rister), a medium into which to carve the runes (usually wood), and paint or pigments to color the runes. The best pigment is a mixture of red ochre and linseed oil, but any red coloring will do quite nicely. Blood was often used in ancient times. The best material for creating a runic talisman is still wood. This may be any kind of wood, but if you wish you can get a type which magically corresponds to the aim of the working you have in mind. You can also take timing into account if you want. Probably the best times for runecraft are keyed to the eight times of the day in the Norse tradition—with sunrise, noon, sundown, and midnight being the most powerful. But in the final analysis the runic tradition remains a highly pragmatic one.

Matters such as substances or the timing used can make as much or little difference as you are willing to allow to them. The simplest rune *taufar* are ones drawn with a pen on a scrap piece of paper. There is no reason to believe that such a talisman will work any better or worse than one labored over for days. The magic is within, not in the outer tools or substances used.

THE WORK OF RISTING A RUNE

Needed for Working

    1) carving tool
    2) stave of wood
    3) red paint, pigment, or dye
    4) pouch or storage place for the finished talisman

1) Preparation

Of course, a good deal of time must be spent in actually designing the form of a rune-tine. The runes provide a precise way of expressing the magical will, and formulas made up of runes must be carefully composed to make full use of this aspect. Examples of a few of the many possible kinds of runic formulas are given below, and many more are contained in other books on rune magic, such as *Futhark*. Once the intellectual work of composing the rune formula is finished, you are ready to go on to the magical working proper.

2) Hallowing

Make the place you are working holy by visualizing the Hammer of Thunar in the four cardinal directions and above and below you.

3) Risting

Carve or draw the shape of the rune-stave, rune-row, or bind-rune while **rowning** (singing) the name of each of the individual runes are they are being carved.

4) Reddening

Paint or inlay the carved shapes with pigment or other coloring (red is always preferred). If you are drawing the staves with a pen you should use red ink. In such cases the **risting** and **reddening** are simultaneous operations.

5) Loading

State in clear and certain terms what the fate and mission of the *taufr* is to be. Visualize the end results of the magical operation—see them as already completed. In the grammar of the loading you might also want to put all the verbs in the past tense to reemphasize this point.

6) Fastening

In order to hold the **loading** to the talisman, trace a ring around the form three times using your right forefinger, knife, or *gand* (magical wand). In doing this visualize a whole sphere around the stave. This sphere will hold the might and main to the object.

7) Hiding

Now that the talisman has been completed it must be hidden or placed in a location where it can most effectively do its work. If it is to affect you personally, it should perhaps be wrapped in a cloth or leather pouch and hung around your neck or otherwise concealed on your person. It may also be stored away or buried in a safe place at the location where it is to do its work.

8) Leaving

Close the working by simply pronouncing the words: *Thus the work is wrought, and so shall it be!*

After the aim for which the tine had been created has been met and the work has been accomplished, you should dispose of the creature in a respectful and careful way. After it has fulfilled its destiny, its *ørlög*, it dies a peaceful death. It may be sent on its way by burning the object, by casting it into a large body of water, or by burying it. A way should be chosen that is most in keeping with the life of the tine. This should be done with reverence and respect. In fact this should be done even if the spell you cast did not work. The fault surely does not lie in the creature you have shaped.

EXAMPLES OF RUNE MAGICAL FORMULAS

1. The simplest, and perhaps the most powerful, kind of runic formula consists of single runes carved and colored with magical intent. You will have already gained experience in this in the creation of the rune-lots for divinatory purposes. These same lots can also be used more actively as magical talismans, however.

2. Bind-runes made up of combinations of two or more runestaves expand and further refine the power and aim of runic formulas. Let us say you wish to gain wisdom of the deep levels of reality, beyond the limits of life and death: You could combine the *áss*- and *ýr*-runes in the shape: . Or perhaps you wish to gain well guided and wise victory in some conflict: You could combine the *týr*- and *sól*-runes in the form . If you wish to win riches but to remain wise and generous in your wealth, you could combine the *fé*- and ***kaun***-runes in the form .

3. The names of Gods and Goddesses transliterated into runes make powerful runic formulas. Examples of these can be found in chapter 5. Magically, *vitkar* would chose the divine power or quality they would like to bring into their lives and make tines carved with the runic formulas of the names of the God or Goddess who provides that quality or power. The runes of these names can also be combined into bind-runes.

4. Certain powerful words from Old Norse or Icelandic also provide for magically potent runic formulas. For example, if we wanted protection we might make a tine from the name of Thórr's hammer *Mjöllnir* (ᛘᛁᛅᚢᛚᚾᛁᛦ), or if we wanted wisdom we could make one from the word for mead, *mjödhr* (ᛘᛁᛅᚢᚦᛦ). If we desired initiation we might do the same with the word for mystery, *rún* ᚱᚢᚾ. Again the runes of these words could be combined into bind-runes.

5. Lines of poetry from the rune poems or from the *Eddas* can also be used as the bases for magical runic formulas. Most lines of the rune

poems can be seen to support a magical intention or affirmation. Use Appendix A to put the Norse text into runes. You will, of course, need an Icelandic edition of the *Poetic Edda* to find many such more lines. An example of such a mysterious poetic line is *œpandi nam* (calling out I took [the runes]), which refers to the exact moment of Óðhinn's runic enlightenment. Transliterated into runes this formula would appear: ᛅᛒᛅᚾᛏᛁᚾᛋᛅᚤ. The original Icelandic for the rune poems can be found in the text of the *Rune-Song* book, forthcoming from Llewellyn. The runes of this and other formulas of its kind could also be combined into bind-runes.

These techniques are further used and in some cases expanded in the magical practice of the Icelandic *galdrastafir* explained in the next chapter.

8 The Magic of Icelandic Galdor-Staves

Working with magical signs or galdor-staves (Ice. *galdrastafir* or *galdramyndir)* is one of the most fascinating areas of Northern magic, yet it is one of the least understood or written about. These signs probably have some of their origins in the obscure pre-runic period, but some have remained popular, at least as curiosity-raising symbols, among post-modern rock bands. For example, the band Psychik TV used Icelandic magical signs on a couple of their albums.

Galdor-staves, as the name suggests, often have something to do with runes. The link with the runes comes in two forms. First the galdor-staves are sometimes made up of complex runic combinations (bind-runes). These are then perhaps further stylized for magical reasons, or just to make them look more beautiful. Second, the actual magical technique of working with these magical signs is very similar to that of working with runes. With runes the magician carves, colors, and sings the right rune songs, while with galdor-staves the magician simply writes or draws the sign, then speaks or sings an incantation or "prayer" formula to charge the sign.

The major historical period of activity for galdor-stave magicians in Iceland was in the Middle Ages and during the Reformation (1000-1750). Although there are examples of such magic from all over the Scandinavian countries, Iceland seems to have preserved or developed the tradition most vigorously.

Over time there seems to have been an "evolution" of this magical practice from strictly runic techniques to that of the galdor-staves. On the other hand, perhaps the galdor- stave tradition is just as old (if not older) than that of the runes and it is just that the signs simply continued being used after formal rune magic had gone into decline.

Most of what we know of the use of galdor-staves comes from a number of manuscripts called, in Icelandic, *galdrabœkur* (books of magic). Only one of these survives completely intact—the so-called *Galdrabók*. This book, along with other similar historical documents, has been translated in *The Galdrabók* (Weiser, 1989). The rest of the material survives in fragments and collections made by humanistic antiquarians or philologists in the 1600s and after.

There were two famous and legendary magical manuscripts in Iceland. One was called *Gráskinni* (Gray-Leather). It consisted of two parts, the first in the regular Roman alphabet and the other in some kind of runic code (Ice. *vil-*

lurúnir, erring runes). Another, and yet more powerful book, was called *Raudhskinni* (Red-Leather). It is said to have been compiled by Bishop Gottskálk. He was bishop at Holar in Iceland from 1497 to 1520. *Raudhskinni* is supposed to have been written in golden runes on red parchment (hence the name of the manuscript). The bishop is said to have been buried with the book. Since he had not taught all of its "heathen" secrets to his living students, the book remains a legendary "lost key" to magical power.

Bishop Gottskálk is only one of the famous magicians of Icelandic lore. In the time just after the "conversion" of Iceland to Christianity, there lived the *godhi* (priest-chieftain) Sæmundur the Wise (1056-1133). He and his sister Holla were said to be "good" magicians, even though they derived their magical power from "heathen lore."

The Icelanders widely regarded magic as being something derived chiefly from their pagan past. In the spells in these books we can see the old Gods and Goddesses being called upon more then half a millennium after their official demise. In fact, it is fair to say the old Gods never died in Iceland.

Besides the magicians of good reputation there were others with darker images. Bishop Gottskálk was one of these. In later times the mysterious figure of Galdra-Loptur (who died in 1722) tried to raise the long dead Bishop Gottskálk from his grave in order to gain possession of the long hidden secrets contained in *Raudhskinni.* But Gottskálk was able to keep his secrets and Galdra-Loptur was left spiritually and mentally shattered by the experience.

Typically these books, or grimoires, were rather like recipe books. They would show the sign or stave and perhaps give the incantation or other prayer formulas to be used in conjunction with the sign. But they never went into the years of preparation the magician would have to go through to make the magic really work.

Magic of the Galdor-Staves

For our purposes here there are essentially three kinds of galdor-staves:

1) *æglshjálmar* (helms of awe)
2) *galdramyndir* (magical signs)
3) *galdrastafir* (magical staves)

HELMS OF AWE
The *ægishjálmar* are often complex cross-like signs with forked ends on the lines of the cross. The simplest form is:

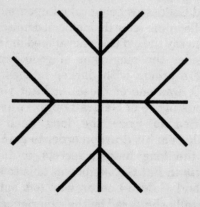

The word *ægishjálmur* means literally "the covering or helmet of awe or terror." In Norse myth it is said that possession of this "helmet" gives the power to strike paralyzing fear into the heart of any enemy and that it can give other magical powers. The *Volsunga Saga* relates that it was a part of the treasure of the Nibelungs. The hero Sigurd re-won this treasure for the Gods and humanity when he slew the serpent Fáfnir.

The helm of awe has been associated with the mythic power of serpents to paralyze their prey—it is a symbol of the outpouring of serpent power from the forehead of the magician. This symbol is really a kind of map or pattern along which power is guided in very specific ways to do its magical work.

An *ægishjálmur* is cast or drawn on an imaginary field representing different levels of reality—all or some of which a particular helm is intended to "cover."

The whole parchment or other medium onto which the helm is drawn represents the entire universe to the magician. These fields or zones represent the objective or outer manifested universe at the outer edges of the parchment or medium; inside this is the subjective, inner spiritual, or psychic universe, while at the very center lies the core self or being of the magician from whom the helm is being cast. The center may also be made to represent the object of the magic. A "map" of how this is visualized on a piece of parchment is shown in Figure 6.

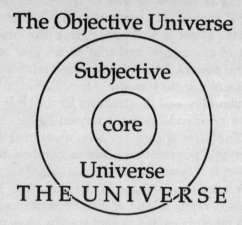

The Objective Universe

Subjective

core

Universe

THE UNIVERSE

Figure 6:
The Visualized Map of the Universe.

These zones can be further divided at more advanced stages of practice. In this, as with most other forms of magic, the aspiring *vitki* should start out simply and progress in measured steps.

On the facing page is an example of a helm of awe which makes use of all major universal zones and most of the main types of signs that occur on the arms of the helm.

With this helm the power is sent outward along the arms. Along the four arms ending in the objective universe the power is highly dynamized and activated by the Y angled terminals and is returned to its source by the ↑ endings. We therefore have manifested conscious (4) power returning to its source. Along the arms ending in the subjec-

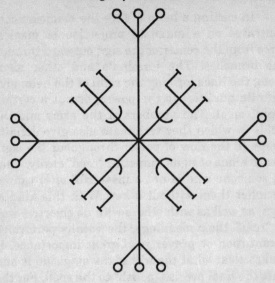

tive universe the power is caught and held in that realm by the ⊤ squared terminals and prevented from diffusing by the ⊺ ends. The power is also held back from returning to the unconscious core of being by the curved lines ψ which trap the power and keep it from returning back in the direction from which it came. The whole then is a map of undifferentiated but balanced core power (8) being blasted out, made manifest and conscious (4), and further empowered in the objective universe; it is returned to the core from the objective universe and sent into a fourfold pattern (manifest and conscious) in the subjective universe. The power is held in the inner world where it feeds the mental and emotional life of the magician. This is a sign of general personal empowerment.

In casting a helm of awe the magician concentrates on a maximal projection of magical force from the center of the sign outward through the branches. The terminals and other signs along the lines forming the radii of the helm give definite qualities to the power, or put a certain "spin" on it. The numbers of the arms and the fields in which they terminate also give definite shape to the flow of power throughout the sign. These kinds of signs cannot be "read" easily. That is, someone who is not a masterful *vitki* cannot decipher them without a key. With this kind of sign, as well as with others with no objective way to "read" their meanings, the vocally performed incantation or prayer is of great importance. It makes clear what the will of the magician is and puts the final precise "polish" to the spell. For the helm to work properly it is, as always, of the utmost importance that magicians themselves are sure in no uncertain terms as to what their intentions are.

Magical Signs

Galdramyndir (magical signs) differ from *galdrastafir* (magical staves) in that the signs seem rooted neither in the tradition of the *ægishjálmar* nor in runic stave forms. However, it might be noted that the term galdor-stave is used for this whole class of signs because the Icelanders seem to prefer the term *stafur* (stave) when referring to such signs of all kinds.

These magical signs were probably originally "discovered" by ancient magicians working intuitively or by a pragmatic trial and error method. Then they wrote down their positive results in their galdor-books. Through these books the results were handed down from generation to generation. From a pragmatic, modern viewpoint this leaves us in one of two positions. We must either follow the signs and instructions handed down to us regarding these signs by rote, or we can strike out anew along the path of "trial and error" used in the ancient past to discover our own "new" signs. This method is not recommended for beginners. This is not so much because it might be dangerous (though it might well be) as much as because its likely rate of failure or deficient effectiveness would be too high. We must remember that the signs and spells found in a *galdrabók* from around 1650 may be the distilled result of 600 or more years of such "trial and error." This distillation process is what makes—or made—those books so valuable.

If you are even to begin to create or discover your own signs, you must learn the principles upon which the signs are based. This requires deep knowledge and understanding of the psycho-cosmology and runology of the North.

The roots of the design of magical signs are probably to be found in arcane psycho-cosmological "maps." But since the signs are so typically "stylized" after their initial design, these original keys are usually totally obscured. Also, although the signs are necessarily produced in two dimensions (on the flat plane of the parchment or paper), in actuality these may represent three-dimensional (or even four-dimensional) figures.

Practice seeing these figures in three dimensions with certain points and lines standing behind or in front of the plane of the paper they are drawn on. This aspect is also present in Cabalistic spirit sigils and other kinds of sigils. Knowledge of these figures helps to vivify the magical power in them in a practical way.

Here are some examples of such *galdramyndir:*

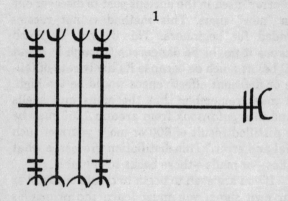

A *kaupaloki*—deal-closer. This sign is used to make successful conclusions to business deals. The tradition says it should be carved on beech wood.

2

A *thjófastafur*—to find a thief. This sign is used to discover the identity of someone who has stolen something from you.

3

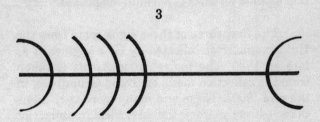

So that you will not be embarrassed in any situation. The tradition says the sign should be made on your forehead with the ring finger of your right hand made wet with spittle.

4

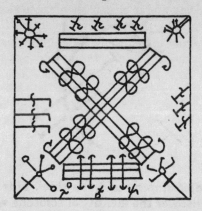

Astros is a sign which can be used as protection against all sorts of harmful magical sendings.

The first three of these signs come from the Huld manuscript collected by Geir Vigfusson as late as 1880! The figure called *Astros* is taken from the collection made by Svend Grundtveig in the mid-1800s. These and many more such signs taken directly from the historical manuscript sources can be found in *The Galdrabók*.

Magical Staves

Bind-runes were known from very early times. It is most likely that the term *galdrastafur* has its origins in the practice of "concealing" powerful divine or magical names or terms by making composite bind-runes out of the runestaves used to write the name or word in question. The resulting bind-rune would then be additionally stylized both to impress it further with the unique will of the magician and to obscure further the key to the bind-rune. The principle of concealing the overt magical meaning of a magical sign or inscription is a powerful key to effectiveness. It is concealed not only from prying, uninitiated eyes, but also from the "meddling" of the conscious mind of the magician. The sign works from beyond the limits of the conscious mind, even though it may be a product of that conscious mind.

A historical example of how this process works can be found in a *galdrastafur* named Thundur. It comes from the collection of Jón Árnason. Thundur is a nickname of Ódhinn and means "one who thunders," or perhaps "the stretched one." The latter interpretation is a reference to Ódhinn's initiatory self-sacrifice by hanging on the World-Tree, Yggdrasill. This is a protective and initiatory aspect of Ódhinn. A galdor-stave formed from this name would be protective and self-transformational—and would give power over one's enemies. The runes used to make up the name in the Viking Age would have been ᚦᚢᚽᛏᛦ. Originally the bind-rune probably looked something like the figure on the next page:

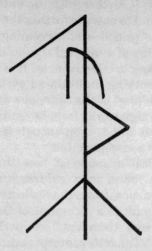

This was then stylized into the form:

Notice the *thurs*-rune was rounded and mirrored on both sides of the upright stave. The *naudh*-rune was made cursive, the *yr*-rune squared, the *úr*-rune made cursive, and, it appears, the *týr*-rune made twice in one-armed fashion (⌐) and once in the two-armed way. In all cases of the *týr*-rune, the normal 45-degree angle of the branch stave was increased to 90 degrees. This historical example and its analysis should provide the modern practitioner with some hints as to how to create original galdor-staves from bind-runes.

One of the main reasons for the prevalence of further stylization of the galdor-staves is the fact that they are written on parchment or paper and no longer carved into wood. The pen allows for more stylistic freedom than the knife or other carving tool. But again the further stylization also hides the obvious meaning from the conscious mind.

In the actual creation of a galdor-stave the younger futhark usually makes the ideal model because most of its runes have a single "main stave" or upright line. It is along this line that the shapes of the runes are made. You may change straight lines to curved ones, double or triple the sign, make mirror images of asymmetrical signs so that they look the same on both sides of the upright, or square off acutely angled rune shapes as you will. The main thing to do with the creation of a *galdrastafur* is to create the feel or image of the kind of power the stave is meant to embody. The bind-rune forms the quasi-rational basis for the sign, but the subjective creativity of the magician provides the emotive keys and the keys of concealment in the subconscious mind.

Once it has been submerged there it can begin a whole new cycle of working.

The magic of Icelandic galdor-staves has its own unique quality. On the other hand, the experienced magician can see many similarities in technique between these staves and the *yantras* (devices) used by tantric magicians in India. There are also parallels with Cabalistic spirit sigils and the *vevers* of Voudoun magical practice. But perhaps the strongest link is with the techniques surrounding the so-called Pennsylvania Dutch hex-signs. It is most likely that both the galdor-stave (especially the various kinds of "helms of awe") and the hex-sign originally belong to the same extremely ancient form of Teutonic magic.

WORKING WITH GALDOR-STAVES

It is sometimes found, especially at more advanced stages of magical development, that the act of designing a working or ritual will in and of itself begin to do the work meant to be carried out through the ritual. However, the actual performance of the rite is often necessary to complete the magical process—to give it "closure."

In any event, planning and designing the stave or sign contains a great deal of magical power itself. When magicians lay out such staves, they are in many ways displaying their knowledge of the universe and their places and ways of acting within the world.

It should always be remembered that the whole sign and the paper on which it is drawn represent the whole universe. In making the sign you are literally redrawing the subtle map of the universe. Each time magicians begin to draw magical signs they must remind themselves that it is just this kind of re-creative act that is being undertaken every time a true galdor-stave is made.

Those who have a great deal of experience in magic will probably see that this kind of galdor has much in common with the theories and practices of the English magician Austin Osman Spare. Perhaps the best and most pragmatic discussion of Spare's magic is contained in the book *Practical Sigil Magic* by Frater U∴D∴. That work contains many more practical hints on how to deal with magical signs of this kind. It might also be noted, of course, that the Icelandic practice of creating bind-runes and stylizing them as magical sigils was already ancient when Spare created his system—perhaps just another example of his theory of atavisms.

RITUAL OF MAKING GALDOR-STAVES

Needed for Ritual
1) parchment or paper
2) pen and ink (black and/or red)
3) two candles
4) straight edge (ruler)
5) table and chair

To these may be added any other items needed to complete the contemplated sign.

1) Preparation
The first stage is the formulation of the magical will—the aim of the sign. The aim must be clear and definite. Once this is decided a stave

must be designed which will bring this willed aim to fruition. Care and focused attention must be brought to bear in the design of the galdor-stave.

Signs may be made at any time but it is generally found that the nighttime hours are most effective for workings intended to affect the objective universe, while the daytime hours may be more effective for workings of protection. Times may also be determined according to lunar phases.

Once the time comes to execute the sign, sit in a comfortable position at a table or desk. Face north if possible. Have two new candles burning to the left and right of the paper or parchment. The paper or parchment itself can be of any size, but usually they are about 8" x 8". A wooden ruler, or better yet a simple strip of wood about 10" long, may be used as a straight edge.

Now spend some time collecting your thoughts and focusing your attention on the sign and the aim of the galdor-stave. You will probably have a "model" of the design which you have created. This can be used for these preliminary meditations, and will, of course, act as a guide to your final magical execution of the sign.

2) Drawing

As you begin to draw the sign think to yourself: "This sign flows through the whole universe. It shapes anew the world with the power of my will." Draw out the sign as smoothly and as quickly as possible—but with full attention to beauty and accuracy as well as to the magical intent of the sign. As you are drawing the sign feel your way into the lines of the sign. See your focus of attention being laid down on the paper—and throughout the cosmos which the paper has become. You are melded into the stave form as your consciousness spreads out through the various zones of the universe encompassed by the sign. The magical aim and intent of the sign will help determine what order the sign should be drawn in. For example, if you are bringing knowledge into your subjective inner world from the outside, or objective, universe, the parts of the sign touching on the objective universe should be drawn first.

The signs may be drawn in red or black ink, or a combination of the two. Black ink is used for signs meant to draw power in, while red is meant for sending power out. A white (paper) or natural (parchment) background is most conducive because it represents the relative "vacuum" into which magicians can project their wills.

After the sign is finished focus your attention on its very center. Concentrate only on the point in the exact middle of the sign. Push outward along the lines—feel the power of the whole sign making itself manifest throughout the world.

3) Singing

After the sign has been completed, set it firmly in your mind and verbally declare the purpose and aim of the sign in an incantational or "prayer" formula. You are free to create your own formulas, or to experiment with traditional ones. *The Galdrabók* is a great inspiration for these. By pronouncing this spell you vivify the sign and give it a very precise and defined power. This is important because the working of the spell should remain under your control at all times. The more exact you are in your intentions, the more likely it is that your will will be fulfilled.

A general formula to be used, or improvised from, would go something like:

After the nature of this stave, that which I will shall come to pass. [Here state in simple, direct and precise terms what your will is] *By all you Gods and Goddesses who live and who have ever lived in Valhalla—Ódhinn, Týr, Thórr, Frigg, and Freyja! So shall it be!*

4) Placement

After the sign is consecrated it should be put in the most advantageous place for it to carry out your will. If you are transforming or protecting yourself, the sign should be kept hidden on your person at all times; if you are influencing a place, the sign should be put in that place or at the entry to that place, and so forth.

EXAMPLE WORKINGS OF GALDOR-STAVES

1) To prevent conflict

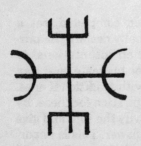

Draw this helm of awe on new parchment in black ink. You may also draw the form on your forehead with your right index finger wetted with water. *"All strife is stemmed between me and whomever I meet."*

2) A dream stave

Draw this sign to help in achieving lucid dreams. (The traditional lore for this sign says it should be carved on fir wood.)

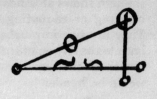

3) For success in business

Draw this sign and keep it under your left arm. Keep its existence a secret.

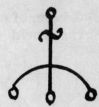

4) For success in court cases

Draw this sign and carry it with you during the legal proceedings. It brings victory in legal matters of all kinds. (The traditional lore states that the sign should be carved on oak wood.)

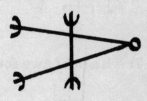

5) To send back any harmful sendings

Draw this sign and wear it in the center of your chest. Any harmful magic being done against you will be sent right back to the sender. Notice that

the sign shows all kinds of symbols for "trapping," blocking or re-routing flows of magical power. They are five in number and they are projected back to the five points in the non-focused nebulous center of the sign—which is the image of the would-be "sender."

6) A helm of awe for empowerment in the world

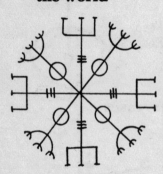

Draw this sign to help empower yourself magically in workings meant to affect the outside world. This sign can then be laid out during any other magical workings as a way of enhancing your abilities to alter the fabric of the objective universe.

7) A helm of awe for inner magical empowerment

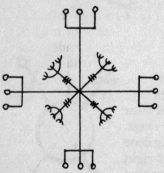

Draw this sign to help empower yourself within. This helm increases inner magical power, which is beneficial in all other workings.

8) For inspiration

Draw this stave for gaining transpersonal levels of inspiration. This stave was developed from a bind-rune of the Icelandic word *Óðhrœrir* (ᚢᛈᚱᛃᛦᛁᛆ), which means "the stirrer of inspiration."

9) For great power

Draw this stave for gaining great personal power—or life force. This stave was developed from a bind-rune of the Icelandic words *mattr* and *megin* ᛩᛁᛏᛆ, ᛩᛁᚠᛁᚼ. These terms can be literally translated as "might and main."

This chapter has served as a brief introduction to a whole and complete school of magical operation which has only begun to be understood again. Use these guidelines in your own practice of pragmatic forms of magic fashioned within the Northern way.

9 Operant Hexology

When German immigrants began to come to this country in the late 1600s through the early 1800s they mainly settled in Pennsylvania, Maryland, Virginia, New Jersey, and New York. They brought with them their native beliefs and magical practices. Most of these immigrants came from southwestern Germany and Switzerland. These folks came to be called "Dutch," which is just an approximation of the name they had for themselves: *deitch* [dye-tch] or *deutch* [doy-tch], German. The "Pennsylvania Dutch" are not in fact "Dutch" but Germans.

Because many of these people became quite isolated in their rural and sometimes mountainous settlements, the old practices they brought with them had the chance to maintain themselves very strongly until fairly recent times.

Among the German immigrants there were many types of religions and views on magic. The "Plain People"—who were basically Mennonites, and who have survived to this day as the Amish —

were not very likely to engage in magic or *brauche* (using), as it is called in the local dialect. But these religious folk were only one small segment of the population. It is more common to find "using" among the (at least nominal) Lutherans, or "nonconformist" sects. But when in need almost anyone might resort to having a *Hexenmeister* "use" for them—even though the highly religious "Plain People" would think it a terrible sin.

The early German settlers brought with them two distinct magical heritages. The farmers and country folk practiced *braucherei* (using) or witchcraft, while in urban areas and in certain utopian communities (such as the one in Ephrata, Pennsylvania) there appears to have been a lively continuity of the Rosicrucian tradition.

Although there have been many famous *brauchers* in the history of magic in the Pennsylvania Dutch territories, there has been none more famous or important than a woman known by the name "Mountain Mary"—*die Berg Maria.* She died in 1819 at her apple orchard in Bucks County. "Mountain Mary" was said to have an owl companion from whom she learned many of her secrets in magic. Owls have been the preferred shape of familiars of *brauchers* at least since that time.

As we will see, the practice of using hexsigns comes at least in part from the pre-Christian magical practices of the ancient Germans.

At one time or another you have probably seen so-called "Pennsylvania Dutch hex-signs" in photographs or books on American folk art, but there has been very little written about the actual use of these signs in practical magic. These signs are usually complex and beautifully designed elaborations of magical signs used by the medieval and ancient magicians from the home regions in Germany. The tradition was, however, handed down with little or no reference to the *origins* of the signs. They were used because they worked.

These signs and the practices attached to their creation were handed down orally from generation to generation. In most places a man could only learn "using" from a woman and a woman had to learn it from a man. Quite often they would only teach their craft to one or two other people in their lifetimes.

As long as the isolated rural society was able to survive, "using" survived more or less intact. But in the early part of this century a combination of unwanted publicity and the increased social mobility ushered in by the Depression together with the Second World War and its socioeconomic aftermath led to the virtual end of the rural, culturally conservative society in which *brauche* had been able to survive for about 200 years. One of the most famous examples of the unwanted publicity is detailed in Arthur Lewis's book *Hex*. This centers on the famous Blymire murder case, which was also used as the basis for the film *Apprentice to Murder*.

Today there are probably no more traditionally trained *Hexemeeschder* (hex-masters) in the region. However, enough of the magical lore has survived and been written down that the aspiring modern hex-master can, with some experimental inspiration, revive this uniquely American form of Germanic magic.

Hex-signs and even some patterns for creating your own hex-signs are available from Jacob Zook's Hex Shops (P.O. Box 104, Paradise, Pennsylvania 17562).

Using Hex-Signs

In theory the magic of using hex-signs works just like the Icelandic magical signs or galdorstaves. The magician plans and designs the sign, executes it with full magical will and intention, and then speaks an incantation over it to "charge" or load it for its particular magical purpose. This combination of graphic execution and oral performance is also a mainstay of the most ancient rune magic, of course.

In his book *Strange Experience*, at least one *Hexenmeister*, Lee Gandee, held that a thought is a thing and that hexing is a projection into the universe of a telepathic blueprint image of what the hexer wants to be materialized. The key is that a *sustained* image must be sent out *far enough* to attract enough energy to make the materialization happen.

To begin with the *braucher* (user) will probably want to stick to known hex-sign patterns, such as the ones found in this or other historical books. However, to become a true *Hexenmeister*, you will have to learn to "read" (interpret) and eventually to "write" (design) your own hex-signs. The design and what you magically put into it will determine how effective the hex will be. Some of the symbolic language of the hex signs is discussed below.

Traditionally the hex-signs were blessed by

means of oral incantations drawn from certain grimoires or manuals of magic used by the German immigrants. Most of these had their origin in Europe; for example, *The Sixth and Seventh Books of Moses*. The Psalms from the Old Testament were also used for this purpose. But one collection of spells called the *Long Lost Friend*, by John Hohman, was first published in America around 1820. It first came out in German with the title *Der Lange verborgene Freund*, which is perhaps most accurately translated *The Long Hidden Friend*. For modern practice these works are still widely available, but magically speaking it might be just as effective, if not more so, to write your own blessing formulas that will exactly put into words the intention you have for the sign.

The ritual of using a hex-sign follows a four-step format.

1) PREPARATION

Be sure you have all of the tools and supplies you need to complete the hex and that you have precisely designed (or found) the hex-sign that will have the result you desire. If you are designing your own sign, the work of planning and thinking it out in every detail will serve as a powerful form of magical preparation for the actual execution of the sign. Just before beginning to draw and paint the sign, spend some time in silence focusing your mind and awareness on the work at hand.

2) DRAWING AND PAINTING (ZEICHNEN)

As you first touch the blank material you are about to transform into a hex-sign, say or think to yourself something such as: "This is the universe (or God); it (or He) surrounds me. The sign I make in the bounds of my mind is laid out according to it (Him)." Draw out the lines of the sign you have planned. (It is often most effective to use the radius of the circle as the unit of measurement in creating any internal geometry the sign may have.) When you are drawing the sign, concentrate on the meanings of each of the geometrical features, as explained below. As you complete the geometrical image, concentrate on the fact that you are pushing your magical signals out over and throughout the entire universe. After the drawing is finished paint the sign with colors selected for their symbolic harmony with the aims of the sign. Some hex-masters think that the colors are purely for the sake of good looks, while others hold that the colors have special magical significance. In any event, the sign must be painted with at least two colors in order to make the design stand out.

3) BLESSING (SEGNEN)

Once the sign is entirely painted, the hex-master holds his hands out over the symbol with his or her palms down and pronounces out loud the blessing or prayer which will "charge" or load the sign with the precise aim the magician has in mind. Hex-signs can and do work their magic on the environment even without the incantation—as incantations can and do work without being "drawn" as hex-signs. But the twofold usage is a powerful combination. The blessing can also be written out on paper or parchment and affixed to the back of the hex-sign. This written formula is called a *Himmelsbrief* (letter to heaven) in "Dutch."

Among Christians it is customary to end such incantations with the formula "In the Name of the Father, the Son and the Holy Ghost," while tracing the sign of the cross in the air over the symbol three times. Pagan practitioners might restore the old formula "By Woden, Willi, and Weh," while tracing the runes appropriate to the working or the sign of the fylfot (卍) over the symbol three times.

4) PLACEMENT

For the hex-sign to work as you would like, it must be placed in the right location. If you want your home to be protected from outside dangers, the sign must be hung on the outside of the house (preferably under a gable). If the sign is for domestic harmony and happiness, it should be hung in a prominent place in the living or sleeping quarters—over the mantle or bed, for example. Certain secret aims call for the sign to remain covered except during certain key times—but these are too complex to enter into at this time.

The Secret Language of the Hex-Signs

There are three major "parts of speech" in the "language" of the hex-signs.

1) The segments or zones into which the universal circle or disk is divided.

2) The symbols and geometrical shapes which give form to the various zones of the universal circle. These come in three main types: the

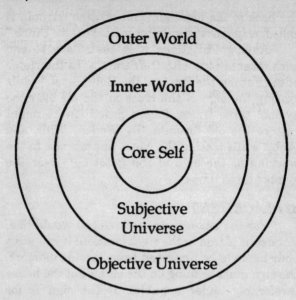

Figure 7:
The Division of a Hex-Sign into Zones

decoration to the bands between the zones, the geometrical figures that often give shape to the body of the sign, and the other symbolic images (usually identifiable with natural objects—tulips, hearts, etc.).

3) The colors which provide at least a nuance of meaning—or "inflection"—to the message of the sign.

Zones of the Hex-Sign

The whole disk or circle of the hex-sign represents the entire universe. It is for this reason that all hex-signs must always be circular or disk-formed. The background color of the circle is almost always white, which represents the pure vacuum of space in the universe. This is a vacuum into which and through which the will of the hex-master can travel freely to work its will.

This disk may be divided into sections or zones representing the objective universe, the subjective universe of the hex-master (or the person for whom the sign is being fashioned), and the core self of the hex-master (or the core intelligence within the universe). Not all hex-signs will have all of these zones, and some will subdivide these zones yet further. A general map of the zones of the typical hex-sign is shown in Figure 7.

The four major ways to divide a hex-sign into zones are shown here:

Those with no divisions have direct influence on the objective universe. They pervade it completely.

Those which only divide the subjective from the objective universes—the inner from the outer world—usually deal with questions of magically affecting one or the other of these worlds directly.

Those which include a core zone within the subjective field, at the very center of the hex-sign, are those which have a strong balancing effect on the very being of the person or persons for whom the sign is being made. In some signs the name of the person or a special personal sigil can be used in this field in order to focus the energy of the sign fully on him or her.

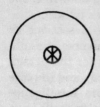

Those signs with only the core field and an outer zone (representing both the inner and outer worlds as a whole) usually address issues of how the core self relates to both the inner and outer worlds as the subject perceives them.

Symbols in the Hex-Signs

The lines or bands dividing one zone of the hex-sign from another have special importance. They define just how the powers inherent in one zone will relate to those in another zone—according to the will of the hex-master.

No imagery on the band indicates that there is a sort of semipermeable membrane between the zones. Power is contained, but it passes freely in both directions, depending on the symbols used within the zones themselves.

Scallops are often described as "waves" in books on hexology. They indicate a smooth and natural interaction between the two zones in question (usually the inner and outer worlds). The power seems to flow more directly from the zone "behind" or "below" the waves.

Chevrons are sharp angles which indicate a direct and effective projection of magical power from behind the points.

Geometrical Shapes

Perhaps the most dominant aspect of most hex-signs is the central, often purely geometrical, shape or figure. These come in basically five major forms: those with no geometrical pattern (usually with one or two pictographic images), and those with three-, four-, six-, or eightfold geometrical figures at their centers.

Those with no geometrical shape usually work purely with the pictographic symbolism, and work directly in the immediate environment of the sign. (The geometrical shapes provide ways for the message or power of the sign to be projected out over virtually infinite space.) Signs with no geometrical shape or center tend to be general blessings, or ones which are intended to have some direct and all-pervasive effect.

Signs with a threefold pattern refer to spiritual matters and help create a dynamic, ever-moving yet ever-balanced, flow of energy.

Those with a fourfold pattern have to do with things of the earth and with matters of prosperity and stability. They give a solid foundation and lead to the actual materialization or manifestation of the things desired.

Sixfold patterns are perhaps the oldest and most popular design for hexes. Six is a multiple of three, so it leads to a higher spiritual reality, but with a high level of stability—as it is also a combination of two and four. The six shows the relationship between God and man, and God and nature to be one of law and order. Another important aspect of the sixfold sign is that it has the ability to interact with the forces which create form and substance directly out of energy. The threefold sign carries this ability in a more basic form.

Eightfold signs are really higher powers of the fourfold signs. They also give great stability and permanence to that which is being asked for, or made to happen. Four- or eightfold signs are most powerful for matters of prosperity, happiness, physical wellbeing or pleasure, sexuality, fertility, etc.

Use of Symbols in Hex-Signs

The symbols used in hex-signs give precise nuance to the general patterns laid down by the geometrical shapes. Each of the drawings has a very specific meaning, and through that meaning the overall power or energy of the hex-sign is shaped and finely tuned to provide the *braucher* with just the results needed. Here are some examples of the most common traditional drawings with their meanings:

The Earth-Star provides all the good things of the earth in stable harmony.

The tulip is a sign of faith, that is *loyalty*—faithfulness. In later times it became a sign of faith in one's self (faith), faith in what one does (hope), and faith in one's fellow man (charity).

The heart is a sign of love. This can be of a spiritual or of an erotic kind. (This difference would probably be best determined by the geometrical pattern in which they were placed.)

The *distelfink* (golden or "thistle" finch) is a sign of good luck and good fortune.

The eagle stands for strength and courage.

 The rooster is for watchfulness—spiritual vigilance.

The diamond is for the four seasons.

 The oak leaf is a sign of masculine qualities of character. Leaves in general are symbols of life and vitality.

Acorns are signs of masculine sexuality.

 Pomegranates mean fertility, prosperity and happiness.

Rain drops are symbols of dynamic water, of nourishment. They can be used in a mundane sense (as in the case of signs meant to cause rain) or in a spiritual sense (as in the case of signs intended to help vivify the inner life of a person).

 The lightning bolt is a sign of storm and stress, of destruction and breaking loose. This can be used to break open the clouds to cause rain—and is also sometimes found on cursing hexes.

Grapes are a sign of female fertility.

 Clover is a sign of modesty and sweetness.

The Key to the Use of Color in the Hex-Signs

As already noted, some hex-masters do not put much stock in the colors used in making hex-signs. But many do, and it would seem to be an additionally powerful magical tool to be used by the modern hex-master. I would suggest that you try making signs in black and white, or in any two complementary colors, and then try signs with a well thought out symbolic color scheme. Try to determine for yourself whether the colors are essential.

White: Innocence, purity, strength against evil, everlasting life, protection against magic, joy. It may also indicate a neutral field of magical action.

Red: Passion, love, strong emotion (love or hate), action, vitality, freedom, kingly power, but also social ostracism.

Black: Death, discouragement, witches, lust, black magic. The color may also be used as a contrast to the neutrality or vacuousness of white in simple contrasting motifs.

Blue: Heavenly love, truth, protection, holiness, beauty, spiritual strength. It is powerful against hostile magic.

Violet: Dignity. power, pride of ownership. Also a sign of suffering and of humility.

Yellow: This color has two very different meanings. It can mean sickness, jealousy, treason, or deception. But it can also indicate sacredness, divinity, the sun, revealed truth, and the love of one's fellow man.

Green: Abundance, luck, fertility, good fortune, the victory of life over death.

Brown: Degradation, sensual pleasure, harvest. But it can also refer to humility and renunciation.

Examples of Traditional Hex-Signs

In reality hexing is a very creative and innovative magical art. If based on sound magical principles the symbols used can be highly personal and particular to the work at hand. The only real limits are the ones placed by the hexmaster and by his or her sense of traditional aesthetics. On the following pages are examples of five hex-signs with explanations or interpretations of the meanings of their symbolism and drawings. More technical details on the construction of hex-signs can be found in Appendix C.

1.

THE DISTELFINK

This sign brings good fortune into the general environment. The *Distelfink* rules over the heart, indicating good fortune reigns in matters of the heart, and the tulip enforces faith and loyalty in love. If you paint the sign, the *Distelfink* should have a yellow (divine love) body, red (emotional) head and wings and a green (good fortune) tail. The heart should be red on the outside and yellow on the inside, while the tulips should also be red and yellow. It should be displayed in the living area of a house.

2.

STRENGTH

This sign draws virility (symbolized by the acorns) and vitality (symbolized by the oak leaves) from the outer objective world and makes them manifest in the inner life of a person. The inner rosette is blue (spiritual strength); the acorns are brown (sensual pleasure); the small leaves coming off the acorns are yellow, indicating a sublimation of sensual pleasure into revealed truth (sexual magic); while the large leaves are half red (physical strength) and half yellow (spiritual strength). The overall pattern is eightfold for the permanent manifestation of the fruits of the sign in the real world. This should be displayed in your workroom or sleeping quarters.

3.

CATALYST

This is a sign to bring great change into your life. Use this type of sign with care and deliberation. The core of the person the sign is made for is anchored in the orderly and protected (blue) rosette. But the inner or subjective world is infused with dynamic spiritual life—four hurling rain drops. The colors of these can be keyed to the kinds of changes you want to come about in your life. The four lightning bolts should be red (action) and yellow (life). The numerology of 4 (worldly) + 4 (worldly) = 8 (stable permanence and balance) leads the harnessed dynamism of the symbols to an orderly result. The scallops around the inner edge make a gentle buffer between the dynamic changes of the inner life and the trials of the outside world. This sign can be kept privately—or displayed in your private room.

4.

MAGICAL POWER

This sign is projected out from a dynamic and balanced threefold spiritual core (blue and white) through an eightfold star (permanent and manifested order) in the inner world. The inner world is also filled with faith and trust (tulips). The star is violet (power) and blue (truth) and the tulips are red (vitality). This combined dynamic core and ordered inner world of power and truth tempered by trust are projected out into the objective world through red (action) chevrons. This sign should be kept private or displayed in your work area.

5.

LOVE

This "classic" Pennsylvania Dutch hex-sign is made to act on the environment of the sign, bringing romantic love and stability into the household. This is a balanced and mature love with emotional and erotic fulfillment. The six hearts (red) bring a balanced emotional love, while the sixfold rosette itself (blue and yellow) brings dynamic yet balanced love on all levels. This could be displayed in the living or sleeping areas of your home.

10 Seith Magic

In the Northern tradition, besides the practice of galdor (or *galdr*), there is also the kind of magic known in Icelandic as *seidh* (seith). In the practice of seith, magicians seek experience outside themselves, seek to submerge their minds and consciousnesses into an otherworldly state—to travel to other dimensions of reality in order to do magical work and to learn things of the world and of themselves. In many ways the practice of seith is identical to the sort of work often called "shamanism" today. In ancient times the *vitki* could shape-shift and gain visions from the realms beyond through the practice of seith. This kind of magic is also concerned with all sorts of natural substances derived from the animal, vegetable (herbal), and mineral (stones, crystals) kingdoms. Quite often the practice of seith also involves sexual activity very much akin to the practices of tantrism or sex magic. It is surely this kind of magic that was the basis for the practice of *wicca*, which is the Old English form of seith-work.

In the ancient traditions of the North it is related how Woden (Ódhinn) was taught the mysteries of seith by the Vanic goddess, Freyja. It is also likely that Woden shared his knowledge of galdor with Freyja. If this is considered, a picture of balance emerges.

Originally the forms of magic that later came to be classified as seith were probably the magical traditions cultivated in the Vanic realm. This was the magic of the farmers and herdsmen, of the craftsmen and smiths, of the musicians and entertainers. Their magic was powerful and unique, and it was probably dominated by female practitioners. As the Indo-Europeans—romantically referred to as "Aryans" by some—moved into Europe several millennia ago, this branch of their magic quickly became assimilated to the local forms of magic native to the folk of Old Europe. The "Old Europeans" are the peoples belonging to the cultures living in Europe before the arrival of the "Aryans."

The runic system of the Odians (Erulians) took this kind of magic into account and learned it (hence the myth of Freyja teaching seith to Woden). The runic system incorporated the doctrines and practices of seith into its structure, and it always formed a part of the curriculum of initiation into the runic mysteries.

In medieval times seith developed a reputation for being "shameful." The negative reputation of seith was a late development, to be sure, and probably one that shows the breakdown of the true heathen culture under socioeconomic pressures from the Christian south. When the days of conversion to Christianity finally came, seith, the magic of Freyja, was singled out for the harshest and most repressive persecution. It is mainly for this reason that so little of the traditions of seith have survived.

Seith-Work

Seith has many things in common with modern neo-shamanism. The recent upsurge in interest in the shamanism of exotic peoples may be rooted in a remanifestation of similar impulses inherited from our own ancestors. If this is so, it might be helpful to investigate our *own* ancestral forms of magic—to seek *within*—before running away seeking for exotic solutions.

Traditional seith rests on three pillars:

1) trance (loss of conscious control of mental processes)
2) slumber (loss or radical alteration of data coming in through the physical senses—sleep of the body)
3) rhythm (use of a rhythmic beat to "ride" while doing seith-work.)

To work seith the you must first achieve an altered state of consciousness. Traditionally this was done with a variety or combination of techniques, including drugs, sleep deprivation, fasting, sensory overload, and even physical tortures, which might be combined with ritual chanting, dancing, and perhaps the playing of some rhythmic instrument. There is no direct evidence that a drum was ever a regular part of the Germanic form of shamanism, but that is no compelling reason why one could not be experimented with today. Once in this "shamanic" trance state, the *vitki* contemplates some mythic landscape, such as that of the realms of Yggdrasill. In the roots and branches of the World-Tree the *vitki* can search for his or her otherworldly mate, magical or protective spirit (fetch), or animal spirit (fetch-animal). In ancient times it is said that the most powerful seidh-men and women could actually send out a part of their souls to take on the shape of a mighty beast to fight their battles while their natural bodies laid as if they were dead. This is obviously an advanced practice, to say the least!

SOOTHSAYING

One of the basic areas of seith-work is **soothsaying,** which is just an archaic way of saying "truth-telling." This is a traditional kind of divination or clairvoyance practiced from the most archaic times.

Soothsaying is very different from divination by runecasting because, in that craft, the analytical part of the mind is used to gain access to the whole realm beyond (in good galdor tradition), whereas with soothsaying a more direct mode of access to actual beings or entities beyond the rational mind is attempted directly. Interaction with the beings known as dises, norns, valkyries, or dwarves, elves, or etins is extremely ancient among the Germanic peoples.

Belief in these beings certainly has one of its roots in the cult of Northern ancestor worship and another root in the lore of the demigods who were attached to certain great or powerful persons, or were the entities responsible for assisting in the teaching of arcane crafts—from galdor and seith to the crafts of smithing and singing. Because of these links, it is easy to·see some kind of connection between what goes on in seith-craft and what was called "spiritualism" in a former time, more popularly known as "channeling" today.

To induce the trance-like state in which you can "say sooth," there are several things to do. First you must be able to get into a state of thought vacuum. Relax your body totally. Relax your body part by part, working from your feet all the way up to the top of your head. Visualize yourself in a sphere of gentle, reddish-pink light. The overall effect should be one of relaxation, but on a deep-down level it should be invigorating and vivifying.

The next step is designed to help open the doors between the seith-man or woman and the natural world—to bring the runester into tune with natural things outside his or her consciousness. To do this, the runester should gather six things—three from the mineral world (for example, a loadstone, a quartz crystal, and a piece of granite) and three from the vegetable world (for example, a branch of evergreen, an acorn, and a leek). When in your receptive, relaxed state, *feel* these objects—let your mind enter into them and meld with them. Concentrate on breaking down the barrier between yourself and these substances.

Now work for a while getting your body in a completely relaxed state. This state is so deep it seems you no longer have any of your five senses. Once you are satisfied with your level of seith-slumber, let a stream of thought open between your conscious mind (hidge) and the receptive mind (myne). It should be as if the myne were a mirror for states of being beyond this realm (Midhgardhr).

Now actually allow yourself to feel as if you were ascending to Llóssálfheimr above. Feel yourself rising from the realm of Midhgardhr along a multicolored rainbow pathway to a realm of brilliant white light high above your head. You can also "fare forth" into other cosmic realms using this technique, but it is perhaps best to fare upward to the realm of the "Light-Elves" before venturing to more obscure worlds.

The last exercise in soothsaying will be to allow yourself to "speak" to some entity in the other realm, and to report what it, he, or she says in Midhgardhr. This report is what constitutes true "soothsaying."

To do this, you allow yourself to rise higher and higher into Ljóssálfheimr. Once you find yourself at a certain place in that world, a door, gate, cave opening, or some other kind of entryway will present itself to your mind's eye. At the same time, beings in that world will approach you. See them, interact with them, attempt some kind of communication. They may or may not be able to communicate with you verbally. It is more likely that images, sounds, and feelings will pass between you.

If one of these beings presents itself as your warden (guardian), make friends with it. The Icelandic term for this entity is *vördhr*—from it we get the term *vardhlokkur* (warlock). Exchange gifts of love and fellowship with it; try to find out its name if you can. At this time you may want to return to Midhgardhr, but if you feel very strong and drawn to do so, enter through the door or other opening before you in the company of your warden.

Ask your warden the question you brought to be answered. Let the warden respond to you. Try to communicate these responses back to Midhgardhr. (If you are working alone, leaving a tape recorder on in the room is a good idea in these exercises.) In this way you will be practicing the most basic form of soothsaying.

Sitting Out

THE NORTHERN VISION QUEST

The traditional rite of sitting out (Ice. *útiseta*) is an act of seith for making contact with your own personal warden or fetch and for gaining ongoing interaction with it. This can be seen as an alternative—perhaps more pragmatic and traditional—to other methods of "gaining the knowledge and conversation of the Holy Guardian Angel."

Útiseta is a kind of shamanic vision-quest working. This type of working can be undertaken for a variety of magical purposes, but here we will explore its use as a way to get in touch with your personal fetch animal.

The fetch (Ice. *fylgja*) is a complex entity attached to persons usually for the duration of their lives. Although it has many forms or aspects, it can also be understood to be a whole being in and of itself. It may appear to the inner eye in three forms. First, the fetch-wife or fetch-man is the spiritual counterpart to the person. This is usually a figure appearing in the shape of a human of the opposite sex. Second, there is the animal fetch. This comes in essentially two kinds: the animal form which most clearly expresses your true inner character, and one which completes or complements your character. This latter shape may even be unpleasant to you at first because it might represent the "shadow side" of yourself. Finally there is a purely geometrical shape in which the fetch might appear to a person.

When you review the animal attributes of the Gods and Goddesses given in chapter 5, you will notice that some even have several such animal symbols attached to them. Odhinn has the eagle, ravens, wolves, horse, and the serpent; Freyja has the wild cat and the sow. The animals help give expression to the divinities, and they can also help express your magical will.

During the course of working your *útiseta* you will come to know what your fetch animal is (assuming there is only one). This will be a great magical tool for self-understanding and self-analysis. Through coming to know your fetch animal, you will come to know your inner self more deeply. Once the animal is identified, it will be able to aid you in inner communication as well as in active magical acts. You will be able to do sendings of magical power through your fetch animal, you will be able to experience unknown things through this part of your fetch, and you will perhaps find ways to use the fetch animal in acts of magical defense.

ÚTISETA

To perform a sitting-out rite, the *vitki* will have to do some careful planning. You will need to have a site picked out. This site must be out of doors and in a place where you are unlikely to be disturbed for a long period of time. The ideal places for such workings are on grave mounds or lonely mountains, or at a crossroads of some kind. Equipment you will need includes: a drinking cup or horn, drink (mead, ale, fruit juice), a vessel to hold the drink in, and a blanket or other piece of cloth about 4 by 4 feet in size. If you are in a wild area, you may also want to bring some different kinds of food to help lure animals to your area, or to a place nearby.

The purpose of the rite is to learn the identity of your fetch animal—is it a hawk, a fox, a wolf, a deer? Or, if you know or strongly suspect what one of your fetch animals is, the purpose of the rite could be to win a closer bond with or experience of that animal.

1) Opening

Walk to the exact site of the ritual. Perform a hallowing working to clear the stead and to make it ready for your working. Take up a comfortable sitting posture on the cloth, with the mead and drinking horn nearby. Facing northward, meditate on your personal character and characteristics. After about 30 minutes, lapse into an inner silence—and hold a solemn vigil of a considerable time (2-3 hours, or more if necessary). The vigil will bring on a certain feeling of "otherness" in a short while. At this time *do not concentrate on the object of the rite;* just allow the feeling of "otherness" to grow—bask in the sensations of its power.

2) Call

At a moment when you feel the power is especially strong, recite the invocatory galdor. You should compose this. If you know what the fetch animal is that you are calling upon, this galdor can be specific to that animal. But more often the *vitki* is trying to find out what that animal is. In that case the galdor can only be a general call. A hypothetical galdor could read:

> Fare forth   holy fetch-deer—
>   come to me creeping,
> that I may   know thy might;
> that I may wax in thy wisdom.

3) Drinking

Pour the mead or other liquid from the vessel into the horn or cup. Hold the horn out in front of you, elevated to the heavens and recite the toast *(full)* to your fetch. This should be a stanza of praise that honors your fetch:

> Hail, holy fetch   high in might:
> thou art my shield,
> thou art my lore-giver,
> thou art my true friend.

Drink half of the horn in one draught and pour the rest onto the ground in front of you just beyond the northern border of the cloth; then place the horn to your right side.

4) Song

Assume a comfortable, relaxed posture and begin to intone the song of final invocation (this may be done out loud, or silently, or in a combination of the two). An example song could be: "Fetch-deer fare thee forth!" Chant this over and over and begin to try to visualize the shape of the fetch before you. (It has always been there.) You may have your eyes closed or open for this. Allow the image of your fetch animal to rise in your mind's eye. It has sometimes been found that an actual animal will make an appearance during the rite. This is why it is best to do this working in an area where animals have the opportunity to come up to you. Continue to chant the song, concentrating on the form of the fetch. After some time of solid contact, lapse into a deep silence.

5) Binding

In a semi-trance state, attempt to communicate with the fetch. Ask it to reveal its name, its lineage, and any other information it might have for you. From this point on, you will be deeply bound to the fetch animal and its natural species. The communication with the fetch animal may take some surprising directions as well.

6) Return

After the contact is complete and the "conversation" is ended, call the fetch animal back into your inner self with the words: "Fetch, fly back!" or something similar. It will return to an area just in front of your chest.

7) Leaving

Close the ritual by simply saying: *So the work has been wrought*—and leave the site.

You may informally contact your fetch at any time after this. Within 24 hours you should perform a blessing in the name of your fetch. In this blessing the animal form is to be worshiped as a personal god-form.

A variation on this ritual formula can also be used to call upon your fetch-deer to appear to you in dreams.

11 The Germanic Role in the Western Tradition

The Germanic or Teutonic peoples have their own special and unique forms of magical practice, such as rune-galdor or seith, but the Germanic influence on the development of what we generally call the Western Occult or Magical Tradition has been very great indeed, especially in the last 600 years.

From the time of the Middle Ages and the Renaissance it was especially the Teutonic or Germanic magicians and alchemists who lent a new spirit of scientific method and systematic thoroughness, as well as pragmatism, to the workings of magic. This was to become the cornerstone of the later occult revival in the late 19th century with such lodges as the Golden Dawn.

During the late Middle Ages there were several Germans among the most important figures in the history of magic. Generally it will be found that unorthodox or liberal ideas and practices—such as magic and mysticism—arise in areas where the authoritarian influence of the Church was weakest. This could be found in the socially and economically free cultures of the north Italian houses of commerce—such as the Medicis and the Borgias. Or it could be found in remote areas such as Germany, Scandinavia, or even England.

One of the greatest contributions to the tradition of magic made in the Germanic territory was the effort made to put magic on a "scientific" basis, to collect the techniques and teachings of magic and to explain them in a rational mode understandable to modern thinkers. The most influential writer and thinker in this regard was probably Heinrich Cornelius von Nettesheim, or Agrippa (1486-1535). Agrippa was a native of Cologne on the Rhine. His monumental *De occulta phlosophia* (On Occult Philosophy) encyclopedically collected most of the known techniques of magic in his day and presented them in a rational way. That work has been the sourcebook for more of the Western Occult tradition than any other single book.

Perhaps the greatest single figure of the magical tradition in the North was Theophrastus Bombastus von Hohenheim, or Paracelsus (1493-1541). Paracelsus was a native of German-speaking Switzerland and is buried in Salzburg, Austria. Paracelsus created a philosophically sound synthesis of the medieval teachings of magic and alchemy. But more than just collecting what was known, he set about proving the validity of the ideas of magic and alchemy in a very scientific way. In many ways, Paracelsus is considered to be one of the fathers of modern medicine. He was in the habit of challenging articles of faith and pragmatically proving or disproving principles based on his own experimentation.

The influence of the Northern mind-set is most obvious in the ways Paracelsus worked and the aims of his workings rather than in the outer symbolism he used. Both Paracelsus and Agrippa applied Germanic thoroughness and systematic rationality to magical methods as never before.

In the realm of mysticism the Germans contributed some of the greatest ideas. Many of these seem to flow directly from the pagan ideology of the Teutons. Perhaps the most important mystic among the medieval Germans was Meister Eckhart (1260-1327). He taught that all people possess an indwelling "spark of the divine" that is natural to them. They only have to awaken to this reality. This was total heresy according to the Church and, although Eckhart was too powerful in his Rhineland home to be excommunicated during his lifetime, he was cast out of the Church after his death. What Eckhart was teaching is not that much different from the Teutonic belief that we are descended from the Gods and Goddesses and that we have suffered no real separation from them other than what we have imagined or have been indoctrinated to believe.

Rosicrucianism

The Fraternity of the Rose Cross was a major school of esoteric thought in Germany during the period of the Northern Renaissance. Rosicrucianism was and is a system that brings together all of the various streams of esoteric thought current in the European Middle Ages. Beyond this it at once "modernizes" these traditions for use in a secular world and creates an organization for the teaching and dissemination of its doctrines.

The first outward signs of the Fraternity of the Rose Cross appeared in central Germany in 1614. The aims of the Fraternity were not merely the enlightenment of individuals, but the reformation or transformation of society.

Rosicrucianism is essentially a synthesis of medieval magic, cabalism (mystical mathematics), and alchemy and thrusts them into the Age of Enlightenment where they were to affect the worlds of both science and statecraft. This system of thought influenced esoteric philosophy from the early 1600s onward.

The Faustian Tradition

One of the most famous figures of Germanic magical history is Dr. Faustus. He is important for the illuminated understanding of what might appear to be a "darker" side of the Northern tradition. He has also become one of the major archetypes of the so-called "Western magician."

There was a historical personage named Georg Faust, who gained a reputation for having sold his soul to a demon for magical powers. This historical figure would have lived around 1530. But it is in the realm of literature, folklore, and magical mythology that the Faustian archetype has its chief importance for the history of Northern magic.

Originally the story of Faust was told and retold to warn would-be sorcerers away from dealings with the "devil"—which may be just another way of saying the human psyche. However, the practical occult literature of the time, contained in the grimoires or magical manuals, shows that the archetype of Faust was indeed being used as a model for magicians attempting to follow the Faustian path.

As European civilization began to throw off the burden medieval evangelists had put upon it, there emerged a new (yet really very old) attitude toward the Faustian path. This is best exemplified in the drama *Faust* by Johann Wolfgang von Goethe, which was completed over the course of his life in the early 1800s. This is the first "Faustian" tale by a "Faustian" man.

The essence of this Faustian path is the will of the magician to give (or "sell") a part of him- or herself to another part of that self—to risk its ultimate loss—in exchange for **knowledge** and **power.** The relationship between this and the Odian path is obvious. But what is also clear is the typical Northern willingness to deal in the realms of misunderstood "darkness" in order to emerge into a wholly new kind of light like none other experienced before.

Originally the tales about Faust had been told as warnings against the un-Christian pursuits of the ultimate evils—of knowledge and power (even immortality). But as the world changed a Faustian Age of Enlightenment began to dawn. This was an age in which the pursuit of knowledge and power became not only acceptable, but good things in and of themselves. Today our technological and cultural advances (such as they are) remain a tribute to the spirit of the Faustian quest for the unknown.

Germany and the Occult Revival

Germany has played a mysterious role in the occult revival of the late 19th and early 20th centuries. Perhaps in a trait dating back to the Rosicrucian period (or perhaps all the way back to the arrival of Hengist and Horsa!), the English have had a habit of finding and placing occult influences in Germany. The Hermetic Order of the Golden Dawn, according to its own teachings on the subject, has its origins with a German lodge called *Die Goldene Daemmerung*. Historians have called this doctrine into question, but the fact remains that the romantic allure of mysterious Germany was strong for the English mystics of the late 19th century.

Really there seems to have been a vigorous exchange of occult ideas and teachings between England and Germany from time immemorial. Remember that Germany is really no more "Germanic" or Teutonic than is England itself.

A more obvious example of an occult connection between England and Germany comes in the form of the *Ordo Templi Orientis* (O.T.O.). This is a quasi-Masonic order with its official roots in England but its magical roots in Germany. The first head of the modern order was the German

Karl Kellner, followed by Theodor Reuss. But control of the order was eventually passed on to the English magician Aleister Crowley in 1922. The O.T.O. really led directly into Germany's most important contribution to the current occult revival—the *Fraternitas Saturni.*

THE FRATERNITY OF SATURN

In the early part of this century a magical order arose in Germany which some say was a revival or continuation of a much older Scandinavian order dedicated to the principles embodied in the demiurge Saturn—which was there identified with Odin. This order is the *Fraternitas Saturni* (Fraternity of Saturn) founded on Thelemic lines in the late 1920s by Gregor A. Gregorius. This order remains the most important exponent of the Western Magical tradition in Germany. The work of the order represents a synthesis of Germanic traditions along with the magical principles of Freemasonry, Templarism, Rosicrucianism, sexual magick, Cabalism, Thelemism, and "Astrosophy," or the magick of the planets and stars.

The Fraternity of Saturn plays much the same role in Germany as the Golden Dawn does in Anglo-American occultism. The order remains a rich storehouse of magical teachings which are only now becoming available in the English-speaking world. Some of these teachings carry a dark aspect, but it is in the darkness where the light of humanity shines the brightest and is most free and manifest as an independent magical agent in the universe. This free interplay of the darkness and the light is a strong feature of prac-

tically all forms of the Northern tradition. Perhaps
it stems back to the original cosmic model of the
Germanic peoples—fire and ice—but for whatever
reason the Northern magician seems to love the
interplay of darkness and light and to take delight
in the state of flux created between them.

The Germanic realms have certainly been no
more influential than any of the other cultural
traditions which have gone into making up the
eclectic mixture which has come to be identified
as the "Western Magical Tradition." The Egyp-
tians, Canaanites, Hebrews, Babylonians, Arabs,
Indians, Persians, Romans, Greeks, and Celts
have all had significant influence. However, it
must also be pointed out that the latter five in
that list, along with the Germanic peoples, all
make up an originally unified cultural tradition—
that of the Indo-Europeans. The role of that great
body of tradition has not yet been fully understood.

12 The Revival of the Northern Way

Because the Gods and Goddesses of the elder Troth are not separate or alienated from our flesh and blood, as long as that flesh endures, so shall They endure. They may sleep or slumber—or perhaps better said we can lose consciousness of Them—but they **cannot die.** For this reason it is somewhat false to speak of a revival—it is really more of a reawakening. Also, as we know, when we awaken from a deep sleep it takes some time to wake up completely. We may stumble around for a while and not be able to think very clearly. Many early attempts at reviving a meaningful Germanic tradition have been failures because we—as a people—were not awake enough yet.

Here I would like to put the whole current interest in Teutonic spirituality or magic into some historical perspective. At the same time I am interested in clearing up as many of the major misconceptions as I can in this short space. Probably the greatest single misconception about the Germanic tradition is that it somehow led to Nazism and that it remains a "fascist" form of spirituality today. The best way to set the factual record straight in a way so that you can make up your own mind is to present a historical sketch of the Nordic Renaissance from around 1100 to the present day.

"History" itself gives us many problems. In reality history is a poetic fiction of sorts. All you have to do is look at fairly factual aspects of contemporary history: Did Lee Harvey Oswald kill John F. Kennedy? The Kennedy assassination is perhaps the most investigated, documented, and analyzed event in history. Yet certainty escapes us. What are the facts? What then is the "truth" about the assassination of Julius Caesar? What are the "facts" of the life of Jesus of Nazareth? Even the external facts elude us and, if they are known for certain, a significant question to ask remains: "So what?" What do the facts **mean?**

For **meaning** we must go to **myth.** Myth is not something which is not true—it is something that (for better or worse) is eternally true. External facts may be unknowable, or if known they may be meaningless or irrelevant; myth is intelligible (with effort), meaningful by definition (often on many levels), and eternally relevant (to the present and future). This is not to say that history is useless. It is a key tool to be employed in unraveling the mysteries we seek, but it is a thankless end in itself. Knowledge of the facts is the most nutritious food with which to feed a highly developed intuitive intelligence. Intuition fed on subjective junk will yield only junk—but feed that same intelligence with hard data and pure gold will emerge.

History of the Germanic Renaissance

The last great temple of the elder Gods was destroyed by Christian missionaries at Uppsala, Sweden, in the year 1100. It is from this date that we can begin to measure the revival of the traditions of those Gods. Of course, the process of Christianization had begun long before that date, and there was really no final "victory" for Christianity even in 1100. The true religion continued for centuries.

It is ironic, yet fitting, that the place where Northern paganism made its "last stand"—Uppsala—was also the site of its first great reawakening. The intervening five and a half centuries (1100-1550) were a time when the ideas and texts of the ancient pre-Christian Northern world were preserved—but in slumbering forms. The Icelanders vigorously and enthusiastically collected and maintained their rich national cultural heritage. The poetry of the scalds was kept alive. This poetry preserved the tales and myths of the elder Gods. Snorri Sturluson wrote his *Prose Edda* in 1222 in an effort to shore up the declining knowledge the Icelandic poets had of their own true traditions. (Note that this was over 200 years after the official conversion of Iceland to Christianity—and that it was only then beginning to decline is a tribute to its tenacity.)

Throughout this medieval period vast amounts of data were being stored and preserved

—much of it in monasteries where it was collected
by monks with an interest in their own natural
traditions—not just those promulgated from
headquarters in Rome. An example of this kind of
material is the *Germania* by the Roman historian
Cornelius Tacitus, who wrote the book in 97 C.E.
This book was carefully preserved, being copied
and recopied by hand hundreds of times by monks
throughout the Middle Ages. Only later (after
1500) would it be fully appreciated for the invalu-
able document it is. It gives us insights into the
values and characters of the Germanic folk in the
Roman Age. Medieval humanists and magicians
preserved the materials which would become
grist for a more powerful mill in the Renaissance.

It is a clear historical fact that in those areas
of Europe where Christianity came late (Scandinavia, England, Northern Germany) it took hold
less effectively than it did elsewhere—and that it
is precisely in these areas where the international
Church was eventually overthrown in favor of
national Churches. This is what happened during
the Reformation. One of the places that accepted
Protestantism quickly was Sweden.

Uppsala remained the true spiritual capital
of Sweden even after the end of official paganism.
It is very likely that a "secret order" of high level
officials around the king remained true to the old
ways. This "order" was disguised within the royal
and even church institutions of the Middle Ages.
It is also possible (if not likely) that this "order"
was one which existed on a virtually unconscious
level by the time the Protestant liberation came
about in the North. We can clearly see how

ingrained and supreme these old ideas were when we see that it was not from the fringe of society or "underground movements" that the impetus for the revival came, but rather from the highest levels of established society. This shows that the old ideas never died; they were only awaiting the opportunity to spring up again.

Johannes Magnus was the first "high priest" of Gothicism—he was also the last Roman Catholic bishop of Uppsala. He was succeeded in his role as chief proponent of Gothicism by Johannes Bureus (1568-1652), who was the tutor and advisor of king Gustavus Adolphus of Sweden.

Bureus was a remarkable man. He was one of the fathers of modern scientific runology (with his contemporary, Ole Worm of Denmark). He was also a magician in the school of Paracelsus and Agrippa. Bureus was familiar not only with Cabalism and Rosicrucianism, but also with the magic and traditions of the more remote regions of his own country. So we see that right from the beginning of the runic revival there was a cooperation between scientific or academic runology and operative or magical runelore.

In the scientific field Bureus made drawings of many of the known Swedish runestones and began to interpret them correctly as ancient Norse texts. Before this, "scholars" had often been baffled by the meaning of these mysterious stones. Hundreds of stones were recorded and interpreted by Bureus in the early 1600s. Some of these monuments disappeared in the meantime, and the records of Bureus are all we have left. (These "lost" stones periodically turn up in farmers' fences or in church walls in which they were used as building materials in the l700s!)

As a a magician Bureus worked with a system which was a combination of the runes and runelore (as he understood it) and Christian Cabalism and the western magical traditions of Paracelsus and Agrippa. The main reason he did not use much of the detailed and profound theological and mythological lore of Germanic origin is that in his day very little of it had been recovered. Even in our time it is a major problem that the very basic lore and mythology is largely unknown to most aspiring magicians. The tendency then as now was to fall back on the familiar rather than forge ahead into the unknown.

The "Gothic Movement" of the l600s was as much or more an expression of the national and political will of the Swedish leaders as it was a true spiritual or magical revival. Although Bureus was, as we look back on his work now, largely "Christian" in his practice, he was an absolute "heretic" as well. Orthodox Christian authorities, whether Catholic or Protestant, were set against him—but he was protected by his close association with the king. Gustavus Adolphus established the office of Antiquary Royal headed by Bureus to be his Gothic "think tank." It was in this period that Sweden became a true world power.

Over the following century the myth and lore of the ancient Teutons only slowly made its way back into the lives of their descendants. From the mid-l600s to the mid-l700s there was interest in the past—but it was largely of a purely antiquarian nature. Humanistic scholars were interested in filling their curiosity cabinets of ideas with quaint and ancient data, so they zealously collected manuscripts and artifacts with no deep understanding of what they were collecting.

Around 1750 a new impetus began on the European continent and in England. The underlying motive for this interest in Germanic heritage was a cultural desire for self-determined authenticity. In the area of the arts the Teutons—be they English, German, or Scandinavian—were tired of the imposition of cultural and artistic values from the Mediterranean world. In the world of art and culture this impetus gave rise to Romanticism, while in the world of politics it led to a renewal of republican/democratic values. The English parliamentarians of the time looked to the ancient Goths as the true model of government to limit the Christian model of the "divine right" of kings. By this Christian theory kings ruled in an absolute and totalitarian way.

In the cultural sphere, this time (1750-1800) was a period when a few visionaries began to understand the concept of pan-Germanic cultural unity. England, Germany, and Scandinavia formed an ancient cultural bond. In pre-Christian times these cultures had shared the same language and the same pantheon of Gods and Goddesses and had had similar political and cultural values. This ancient bond still held the heartstrings of these nations—but now in an almost hidden or secret way.

Following 1800 Romanticism came into full swing in the Germanic areas. Romanticism is essentially the desire to turn inward to find what is valuable and great in life. It is a turn toward feelings and intuition. In individuals this is reflected by interest in the interior life—even in the night side of nature. In nations it is often reflected by an interest in the past heritage of the folk.

It was again in Sweden where Nordic ideals most strongly influenced this movement. But this time, instead of coming from the royal house, it came from philosophers and artists. This up-welling of the movement from more popular levels is typical of the Romantic urge.

In 1811 the author Jacob Adlerbeth founded the *Gotiska Förbund* (Gothic League) in Stockholm among a group of artists, poets, and philosophers. Among its members were the poets and social reformers Erik Gustave Geijer and Per Henrik Ling. The aims of this league included the revival of an ancient Germanic spirit of freedom and promotion of national independence. It was also interested in researching ancient Norse literature and cultural traditions. This research would, of course, help refine and inform the movement in its more revolutionary aims.

Not long after this, in 1815, the *Manhemsförbund* (League of *Manhem)* was founded in Stockholm. *Manhem,* or the "World of Man," is a Romantic name for the North based on the Old Norse *Mannaheimr.* The author C. J. L. Almqvist began the *Manhemsförbund* as a true initiatory secret society or lodge. The aim of the *Manhemsförbund* was more the transformation of the individual than that of society. The mysticism of Emmanuel Swedenborg (1688-1772) greatly influenced Almqvist.

These societies and orders were not yet able to cause a large-scale breakthrough in the Germanic Renaissance, largely because the basic data necessary to inform the Renaissance was still lacking. It was left to the German "academic Romantics"—chiefly the brothers Jacob and Wilhelm Grimm—to put the future of the Germanic Rebirth on a firm foundation. The Grimms researched Germanic antiquities and set up formal studies of every aspect of ancient Germanic culture—religion, mythology, language, law, and folklore. The Grimms were Romantics—or "Germantics"—who wanted to show that the Germanic culture and intellectual world was every bit the equal of the Greco-Roman and Judeo-Christian. It was just that Mediterranean cultural imperialism had suppressed the old Germanic ways. The time had come to let the old suppressed material rise up and throw off the foreign overlay so that the people could again be true to themselves.

Jacob Grimm first published his *Deutsche Mythologie (Teutonic Mythology)* in 1844, and the two brothers together collected and published their *Kinder- und Hausmärchen* ("Fairy Tales") from 1816 to 1818. These, and a host of other less celebrated works, put the future of the Germanic Renaissance on a firmer foundation than had ever been the case before.

This phase of the Germanic Rebirth (1800-1850) was characterized by a romantic longing for the lost values of the past. It was largely an "ivory tower" movement active among artists, thinkers, and academics. It was a movement of the soul and emotions, but it was also a time for the laying of

firm intellectual foundations. But even if it has its
origins in the sphere of artists and academics, its
inspiration came directly from the folk, and the
fruits of the academics' labors were intended to
find rest again in the hearts of the people.

In Europe during the middle of the 19th century the cause of **nationalism** was identified
with liberalism—the urge to freedom. The force of
conservatism attempted to preserve—conserve—
the way things were. At that time the status quo
was a Europe ruled by absolute monarchs (based
on the Christian divine right of kings) and split
up into political states which did not conform to
national realities. The Germans, for example,
were divided up into dozens of kingdoms, duchies,
and principalities; there was no unified German
state in harmony with the culturally unified German **nation**—that is, the German-speaking people of central Europe.

The second phase of the modern Germanic
Rebirth (1850-1900) might be called the liberal
and utopian phase. By this time at least some of
the real values and ideas of the ancient Teutons
had begun to filter down to a more popular level.
The Nordic or Germanic ideals became more and
more appealing on a broad popular level. The ultimate Germanic mythic hero—Sigurd or Siegfried
—became a new pattern of human development.

Artists and thinkers such as the Early
English socialist and author William Morris used
Germanic mythology and cultural history as a
model for utopian solutions to the problems
brought on by the Industrial Revolution. Even the
German Friedrich Engels, who co-wrote the *Com-*

munist Manifesto (1848) with Karl Marx, wrote a Siegfried drama entitled *Der gehörnte Siegfried* (The Horned Siegfried). The Teutonic past was being seen more and more as a model of social and religious order which had worked in the past, and which could work again if the right combination of keys was found to unlock the deep secrets of the past.

In Germany the dominant figure in the Germanic Renaissance during the last part of the 19th century was Richard Wagner (1813-1883). His interest went beyond merely using Germanic themes for entertainment purposes in his operas—or "total works of art," as he called them. Wagner was essentially a social and cultural revolutionary who used the medium of art as a catalyst for change. Essentially Wagner was a progressive revolutionary who attempted to "redeem" the world from materialism through his symbolic "total works of art." The enlightened, some say "mad," King Ludwig II of Bavaria tried to help him in his aims. But Wagner's program was deeply flawed due precisely to the trait that makes his accomplishments great art—it was all too original. His own genius often got in the way of just letting the ancients speak through him. Also, of course, he was *used* to ends he never intended by the National Socialists and their ilk.

It is little known but true that the idea of "Scouting" has its origins in the later 19th-century English longing for the vitality and spirit of the Anglo-Saxon past. There was an enormous "youth movement" in England, as well as in Germany, which pointed in the direction of creating rural utopian communities based on vital and natural ideas of the national past. These communities would then become the bulwark of a new culture once "civilization" had failed. These ideas continued to be strong in England until the time of World War II.

For the late 19th- and early 20th-century phase of the Germanic Renaissance, the ideas of returning to nature, social reform, and peace on the national and international levels, all in the context of ancient and traditional national values, were really the dominant ones. These were, unfortunately, perverted in the early 20th century—which set back the true cause of the Rebirth by a century, I would estimate.

During the early 20th century the Germanic Rebirth began to take an ugly turn. As can be seen from what has gone before, the movement was hardly mature. This childlike movement was, however, faced with some enormous cultural and political problems. Europe was plunged into World War I, the Communist revolution in Russia, and widespread economic chaos. The immature response of the movement was to abandon its long-held ideals of National liberalism and progressivism for an authoritarian racism. Racism is an immature understanding of nationalism. One does not have to hate others as a sign of loving one's self. In fact, if hatred of others is a hallmark of a movement, it is probably because the members of that movement really hate themselves. True "nationalism" involves respect for and assumed freedom and independence of other national folk groups.

Germany and Austria saw the rise of dozens of neo-Germanic groups, orders, societies, and churches, and hundreds of books and periodicals dedicated to the cause, in the time before the First World War. But these dramatically multiplied after that war. It was on this virtual tidal wave of popularity that the Nazis rode into power in 1933.

In the early 20th century there was the Guido von List Society (and its inner *Armanen Orden)* and the runic circle around Friedrich Bernhard Marby. The old liberal and utopian tendencies were being bled off into "reactionary" and conservative directions by pressures from the right and left. A powerful and popular movement that had swelled up from the grassroots was at a loss for guidance. In 1933, when the National Socialists took power, the movement as a growing cultural phenomenon began to die. What the Party could not absorb it destroyed. But because, for propagandistic purposes, they marched under the banner of "Germanism," and because in the years subsequent to their defeat all that they had touched came to be identified as absolute evil, the whole subject of "Germanic spirituality"—once so broad and deep that millions sought it and millions found it meaningful—was tarred with the brushstroke of "Nazism." This is unfortunate and very false. The Nazi interlude was in actuality 12 years in which the "Germanic Renaissance" was wrested from the hands of the people and put in the hands of the state. As yet the people have not been able to win back the banner of the movement from this misconception. The only way it can be rewon is if people understand the great historical process that has been going on for at least 1000 years.

The Northern tradition of magic has for some time suffered under two kinds of problems. First there was a vast ignorance concerning its existence and its deep roots in the "folk-soul." The native organic traditions of the Europeans, be they Celtic or Teutonic, were submerged under the false cultural prestige of the Greco-Roman and Judeo-Christian worlds. This burden was only thrown off with the help of the scholarship and magical work of the past 200 years. This research showed what vast natural, authentic magical and religious traditions are to be found in our own cultures. The second problem has been the misguided use of these traditions. In this century we have seen how Germanic symbolism has been used not to liberate but to enslave and destroy. This does not necessarily have anything to do with the true practice of Northern way, but it does show the incredible storehouse of power available in its symbolism.

The Nazis did not invent neo-Germanicism —they subverted something that was already strong for their own political purposes. Unfortunately, many would-be revivalists of Germanic culture, religion, and magic are all too enamored of the Nazi mythos and mystique. The National Socialists did not advance the cause of Germanicism—they set it back at least 100 years.

The ancient Teutons were freedom loving, individualistic, tribal folk who would have had little in common with the totalitarian, collectivist state conjured up by Hitler and his associates—no matter how it was "packaged." Most current works purporting to connect Nazism with sinister cosmic plots or Satanic conspiracies are usually just the products of their authors' lurid imaginations and fantasies.

After the Second World War serious interest in Germanic spirituality was slow to reemerge mainly due to the "bad press" the subject received at the time of the war and following.

But great ideas with a history of centuries of struggle against the odds could not and cannot be kept down by these "image problems." In the 1950s an obscure Australian Odinist, A. Rud Mills, produced a series of books attempting to revive Odinism, while in Germany Karl Spiesberger was reviving the runes and rune magic.

Nevertheless it would really take a full quarter of a century from the end of World War II for serious attempts to renew the Germanic Renaissance. In the early 1970s a variety of groups were founded in Germany, England, Iceland, and the United States. By 1980 the Rune-Gild was founded as an effort to renew traditional runic methods of initiation.

From this short sketch of the long history of Germanic revivalism, I hope it has been made a bit clearer that this idea is not a fad of any kind or a flash in the pan—it is a long-standing, deeply seated urge of our folk to return to their spiritual and cultural roots. It has welled up time and again—but each time the emotional or passionate energy has been strong, the authentic knowledge-base needed to channel those passions in a positive way has been lacking or deficient. Now for the first time in history there is the possibility of linking an authentic knowledge-base with the passion for renewal. But this work remains one of the most difficult cultural tasks of all time.

The Future

The time has come for a grand unification of all of the streams of the Germanic Renaissance that have gone before. The time has come to return to some of the spiritual roots of the early 19th century with its artistic Romanticism, and to the essence of the late 19th-century movement with its social conscience and urge to form independent communities based on true principles of the Germanic heritage. In the future the Germanic revival can no longer be burdened with the reputation thrust upon it by the actions of those who betrayed the cause in the past.

Right now the Northern way is much like the sapling of an oak tree. It has grown from an acorn inherited from days of yore, but it is essentially a new and flexible organism. The Germanic tradition is every bit as rich and varied as the Hermetic or Cabalistic. At this stage in its rebirth there is a great opportunity—and a certain danger inherent in that opportunity—for individuals and groups to contribute to the shape of the final oak tree that this tradition will again become. The danger is that the young tree could be deformed through ignorant and unwise attempts to alter its natural growth. It has survived at least one of these—the fiasco of 1933-1945—but it remains unknown as to how many more such episodes it could take. If the true way is to fulfill its destiny—its wyrd—it will have to be guided by a wise and knowledgeable folk.

> *Runes again are risted,*
> *a worthy word is rowned,*
> *the gods are risen up all-wroth:*
> *Take now the lead ye lords,*
> *and load the horns ye ladies;*
> *in the troth lies the truth.*

Appendix A

On the Transliteration of Icelandic into the Runes of the Younger Futhark

VOWELS

a/a	ᛅ
ö	ᛅᚢ or ᛅ
ø	ᚢ or ᛅᚢ
jö	ᛁᚢ or ᛁᛅᚢ
ei/ey	ᛅᛁ
æ/œ	ᛅ or ᛁ
æn/œn	ᚠ
o/ó	ᚢ
u/ú	ᚢ
e/é	ᛁ
y/ý	ᚢ
i/í	ᛁ

CONSONANTS

b/p	ᛒ
(c) (q) k/g, ng	ᚴ
l	ᛚ
m	ᛘ
n	ᚾ
medial and initial r-	ᚱ
final -r	ᛦ
s/z	ᛋ
t/d	ᛏ
v	ᚢ
f	ᚠ
j	ᛁ
h	ᚼ

Nasals (m/n) before dentals (d/t) are generally not written, thus *brandr* = ᛒᚱᛅᛏᛦ .

Runes are generally not doubled, thus Ódhinn = ᚢᚦᛁᚾ ,even when they belong to two different words.

All of these rules may be violated for magical purposes.

Appendix B

On the Carving of Runes

It is certain that wood was the original material into which runestaves were carved. The technical runic terminology makes this quite clear. The most obvious example is the word "stave" itself (ON *stafr;* Old High German *stab;* Old English *stæf),* which literally just means stick or staff (of wood). The medium quickly came to mean same thing as the message (in this case). So the word "stave" took on all the meanings of "rune." Even in later times when runes and rune-like signs were used in medieval and Reformation-Age magical grimoires, the term used for "writing" these "staves" with pen and ink was related to the original word for "carving" or "cutting."

The archaeological record clearly shows various ways of carving runes into a wide variety of materials—wood, bone, metal, and stone. Different types of risters (carvers) or saxes (knives) are usually employed for carving into the various materials, but here we will concentrate on the rister used to cut into wood.

Archaeological findings make one thing quite clear, and that is, despite what you may have read elsewhere, the runestaves were almost always cut across or against (seldom with) the grain of the wood. That may be one reason why they generally avoid 90-degree angles. This is done so that the lines of the runestave will not get lost in the grain of the wood. When carved in this way the stave is clearly legible even without coloring.

A Stave Carved Against the Grain

You should now set about practicing rune-carving. Get a good supply of wood and, with your rister, experiment with various methods of rune-carving. Pragmatically an X-Acto® knife is ideally suited to most rune-carving needs, but a sharp pointed instrument (such as an awl) or other carving instrument also does an excellent job. You will see that you can easily, and quite quickly, scratch the runes into the wood. This method is preferred if no color is to be added. But for more elaborate purposes you will want to cut the rune-shape out more smoothly and carefully with the sharp blade of your sax, leaving a nice groove in the wood into which the color will be laid. Really, the only limit placed on technique is the imagination and ability of the runester—the archaeological record demonstrates this to us well.

Appendix C

On the Construction of Hex-Signs

Although strictly speaking hex-signs can be very simple to make, they also can potentially be quite complex and involved. This magical craft can be ideal for those with some significant artistic or technical talent. Especially when the sign is to be displayed either inside or outside someone's home, the sign's qualities of beauty become an important consideration. Therefore great care must be taken in the design and construction of the sign for both magical and purely esthetic reasons.

To construct most signs you will need a round, flat piece of wood or pressboard, a compass for drawing circles, a straight edge or ruler, some paper, scissors, and paints to color the sign. The size of the sign will be determined by how the sign is to be used and where it is to be placed. The average size will be about 12" in diameter, but some to be placed outdoors can be much larger.

Note that hex-signs can also be drawn on paper in any size using only black and white (or color as need be). They can just as easily be displayed in that form. However, the standards of beauty cannot be given up. The care needed to construct them is part of their magic. I would suggest beginning experiments in hexing with simple constructions so that the technical aspects do not get in the way of your magical aspirations. As your technical skills improve you can expand your magical expertise as well.

Here I will follow a step by step construction of the hex-sign for Magical Power shown in chapter 9 on page 156. In this as in all signs you will make the zones first—remembering to concentrate magically on the significance of what it is you are doing—and then work your way from the inside out or from the outside in, depending on

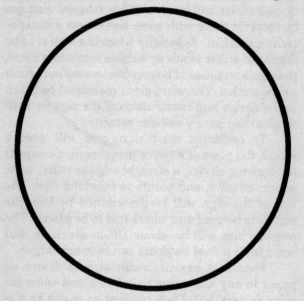

the nature of the hex you are working.

1) Paint the surface of your sign a bright shining white. This is perhaps best done with spray paint. Be sure the surface of the sign is very smooth. You now have a pure white surface to work on.

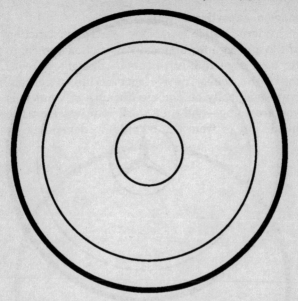

2) Now with a compass, or with a string and pencil anchored in the center of the sign, draw the circles or rings that will make up the zones of the finished sign.

3) Next complete the design in the center. First do any geometrical features, then any pictographic ones. Realize that magically this is the core.

4) Now add the geometrical features of the next zone out—the zone of the inner personal world.

5) Next add the pictographic features in the same zone. Patterns for symmetrical pictographic symbols such as tulips, hearts, stars, etc. can be made by drawing half of the symbol on a piece of paper, folding it, and cutting out the symbol with scissors. You will then have a perfectly symmetrical image of the symbol in the exact size you need. These could be reused, if necessary.

6) **Finally add the design in the outermost circle, or zone of the "outer world." This will complete the construction of the sign itself.**

As far as painting the sign is concerned, you could paint it as you go along—zone by zone—or you could wait until you have the outlines drawn in with a pencil and paint it all at once. If you opt for the latter method, paint the sign in the same order you drew it—from the inside out, or from the outside in.

When the sign is complete, and the ritual for blessing it is finished, hang it or put it in the place where you want it to do its work. Some signs are fixed by means of a nail through the center. In case you want to do this, a hole should be drilled in the center before driving the nail. This will avoid splitting the wood with the nail. The nail can become a further conduit for magical power flowing through the symbolism of the sign.

Glossary

This glossary of technical words used throughout the text of this book indicates the exact definitions of words that might be used in unfamiliar contexts. Here the Old English (OE), Icelandic (Ice.), or Old Norse (ON) terms from which some of these technical terms are ultimately derived are also provided. All foreign (non-modern English) words are followed by approximate phonetic transcriptions in square brackets. An underlined <u>th</u> indicates a voiced "th" as in "then" or "other," while "th" not underlined indicates a voiceless "th" as in "thin."

ægishjálmur [eye-yis-hyalmur]: Literally this means "helm of awe." In mythology it is said to be part of the Nibelungen hoard. In Icelandic magic it is a type of geometrical cross-like magical sign with several arms. They can be constructed for any purpose.

ætt [ate], pi. *ættir* [ate-ir], see *airt*.

airt, pl. airts: The eightfold division of the sky, and the divisions of the futhark into three groups of (originally eight) runestaves.

Æsir (pl.) [ay-zeer] *Áss* (sg.) [awss]: The Gods and Goddesses of consciousness in the Teutonic pantheon, governing the powers of sovereignty and physical force. Called Ases [aces] in English.

209

Asgard: The enclosure of the Gods, the realm where the Gods and Goddesses exist. (ON *Ásgardhr* [ahz-gar<u>th</u>ur])

athem: The "breath of life," the vital force of life borne in the breath. (OE *æthm* [ay<u>th</u>m])

bind-rune: Two or more runestaves superimposed over one another, sometimes used to form galdor-staves.

blessing: The act of sacrificing and distributing the powers of the Gods and Goddesses in Midgard. (OE *blōtan* [bloht-an] and *bletsian* [bletz-yan], to sacrifice)

boast: A ritual drinking to the honor of a God, Goddess, or ancestor, or drinking to seal an oath for future actions. Also, a "toast." (OE *beot* [bay-ott])

brauche [BROWKH-uh]: Pennsylvania Dutch term literally meaning "to use (magic)."

braucherei [BROWKH-er-eye]: Pennsylvania Dutch term for the practice of magic. Also called *hexerei* [hex-er-eye].

brauchbuch [BROWKH-bookh]: Pennsylvania Dutch term for a grimoire or manual of magic. The most famous of these is John Hohman's *Long Lost Friend*. Another term used is *hexebuch* [HEX-uh-bookh].

call: The part of a ritual in which the divine forces to take part in the blessing are invoked.

dis, pl. dises: Ancestral female divinities to whom Winter Nights and Disting are holy. (ON *dís* [deesl; *dísir* [DEEZ-ir])

drinking: The part of a ritual in which the liquid charged with the divine forces is ingested by the gathered folk.

Elder: A recognized "priest," or "priestess" in the Ring of Troth. (OE *ealdor* [ay-aldor])

etin: A "giant," which is a living entity of great age, strength, and often great occult knowledge. (ON *jötunn* [yott-un]; *jötnar* [yott-nar])

fetch: A soul aspect which appears to the mind's eye in a variety of forms—as a person of the opposite sex (fetch-wife or fetch-man), an animal (fetch-deer), or even in a purely geometrical shape.

fetch-deer: The soul-aspect which appears to the mind's eve in the shape of an animal. In this formula. the "deer" refers to all animals in general. From Ice. *dýrfylgja* [DEER-fil-ya]: animal fetch.

folk: 1) The Teutonic or Germanic nation (all people of Teutonic heritage, German, English, Dutch, Scandinavian, etc.). 2) The people gathered for a holy event.

formáli, pl. *formálar:* Ice. Formulaic speeches used to load ritual actions with magical intention.

frith: The true Germanic word for "peace," which carries with it the implication of "freedom."

galdor: 1) A magical incantation or mantra. 2) A form of magic which often uses runestaves as a method of obiectifying verbal contents and thus objectifying magical intent. (ON *galdr*, pl. *galdrar)*

galdor-stave: A magical sign which may or may not have its origin as a bind-rune. Used as a focus for complex magical operations. (ON *galdrastafr*, pl. *galdrastafir.)*

galdramyndur [GALD-ra-minn-dur]: Literally this means "magical sign." It is a magical sigil created for pragmatic purposes.

galdrastafur [GALD-ra-stav-ur]: Literally this means "magical stave." Originally they were made up from bind-runes which were then stylized for magical purposes.

gand: The magical wand. (Ice. *gandur)*

giving: The part of a ritual in which the remainder of the charged liquid not consumed by the gathered folk is returned to the divine realm. Also called the "yielding."

hallowing: The part of a ritual in which the space

where the ritual is to be performed is marked off from the profane world, made holy, and protected.

harrow: 1) An outdoor altar usually made of stone. 2) A general term for the altar in a true working. (OE *hearg* [hay-arg])

hexemeeschder [HEX-uh-maysh-der]: Pennsylvania Dutch term for a sorcerer. Literally it means "master of hexing."

hex-sign: A round symbol painted with magical motifs which act as an elaborate talisman or amulet.

hidge: The cognitive part of the soul, the intellect or "mind." Also called hugh. (OE *hyge* [hewg-uh])

himmelsbrief [HIMMEL-s-breef]: Pennsylvania Dutch term literally meaning a "letter of heaven." In the mythology they were supposed to represent epistles of Jesus himself.

holy: There are two aspects to this term: 1) that which is filled with divine power, and 2) that which is marked off and separate from the profane.

hyde: The quasi-physical part of the soul which gives a person shape and form. (ON *hamr* [hahm-er])

leaving: The formal closing of a ritual.

loading: The part of a ritual in which the sacred power that has been called upon is channeled into the holy drink.

lore: The tradition in all its aspects.

lot: A runic talisman (rune-tine) used for divinatory purposes.

love-seith: Sexual magic. The use of sexual symbolism or energies in seith-craft.

lyke: The physical part of the soul-body (psychophysical) complex. Also called lich. (OE *líc* [leech])

Midhgardhr [MITH-garthur]: the dwelling place of humanity, the physical plane of existence. Also, Mid-yard, the enclosure in the midst of all. (OE *Middangeard* [MIDD-an-yeh-ard] Meddlert.

mood: The emotional part of the soul closely allied with the wode. (OE *mod* [mode])

myne: The reflective part of the soul, the memory: personal and transpersonal. (OE *mynd* [mew-nd]; ON *minni* [minn-ee])

ørlög: ON Literally analyzed this means "primal layers" (primal laws)— the past action of an individual or the cosmos) that shapes present reality and that which should come about as a result of it. Its root concept is the same as English **wyrd** or weird.

reading: The part of a ritual in which a mythic-poetic text is recited in order to place the gathering into a mythic time/space, to engage in the mythic flow of timelessness.

rede: The part of a ritual in which the purpose of the working is stated.

rister: A special pointed tool used to carve rune-staves.

rown: A verb meaning basically "to whisper secret things" (that is, runes). It is the verb-form of **rune.**

runecasting: The operation of runic divination.

runecraft: The use of runeskill (esoteric knowledge) for causing changes in the objective environment.

runelore: A general term for teachings about runes both exoteric and esoteric.

rune-skill: Intellectual knowledge of runelore.

rune-stave: The physical shape of a runic character.

runester: From ON *rynstr* [rinn-ster], "one very skilled in runes." General term for someone involved in deep-level runic studies.

rune-thinking: Runic meditation.

rune-wisdom: Ability to apply rune-skill to deep-level visions of the world and its hidden workings; runic philosophy.

rune-work: The willed effort and process of self-transformation using runic methods.

sending: The magical technique of projecting runestaves and their powers out of the self into the world to do their rightful work.

seith: A kind of magical technique contrasted with galdor. Seith involves attaining trance states and often involves sexuality. The kind of magic taught to Ódhinn by Freyja. (ON *seidhr* [sythe-er])

signing: The magical technique of tracing rune-staves in the air to "rist them in the world."

soul: 1) A general term for the psychic parts of the psycho-physical complex. 2) The postmortem shade. (OE *sawl* [SAH-wel])

stall: An indoor altar, especially one that is backed up against an interior wall. (ON *stalli* [stall-eel])

taufr [tow-ver]: ON. 1) Talismanic magic. 2) The talismanic creature or object itself.

thurs: A "giant," opponent of consciousness. From Ice. *thurs* [thursh], pl. *thursar* [thursh-ar].

tine: A talisman.

troth: Religion, being loyal to the Gods and Goddesses and cultural values of the ancestors. (ON *trú* [troo], OE *treoth* [tray-oth])

true: Adjectival form of "troth," can mean "loyal." A "true man" is a man loyal to the Gods and Goddesses of his ancestors.

Vanir (pl.) [VAHN-eer] *Van* (sg.) [vahn]: The Gods and Goddesses of organic existence in the Teutonic pantheon, governing the realms of organic production, eroticism, wealth, craftsmanship, and physical well-being. Called "Wanes" in English.

wight: A being or entity of any kind with some living quality.

wode: An emotive, synthesizing part of the soul which brings various aspects together in a powerful and inspired way. Related to the mood. (OE *wōd* [wode], ON *ódhr* [OH-ther])

world: The psycho-chronic human aspects of the manifested universe. (OE *weoruld* [WEH-oruld], the age of a man.) The cosmos.

World-Tree, see Yggdrasill.

wyrd: The process of the unseen web of synchronicity and cause and effect throughout the cosmos. Same as weird.

Yggdrasill [igg-drah-sill]: The framework of the cosmos made up of nine major realms or worlds and the 24 roadways and streams interconnecting them. The word means "the steed of Yggr (= Ódhinn)" or "the yew-column."

Bibliography

Bauschatz, Paul C. *The Well and the Tree*. Amherst, MA: University of Massachusetts Press, 1982.

Byock, Jesse, tr. *The Volsunga Saga*. Berkeley: University of California Press, 1990.

Dumézil, Georges. *Gods of the Ancient Northmen*. Translated and edited by E. Haugen. Berkeley: University of California Press, 1973.

Ellis, Hilda R. *The Road to Hel*. Cambridge: Cambridge University Press, 1943.

Flowers, Stephen E. *Runes and Magic*. Berne: Peter Lang, 1986.

Flowers, Stephen. *The Galdrabók: An Icelandic Grimoire*. York Beach, ME: Weiser, 1989.

Flowers, S. Edred. *Fire and Ice*. St. Paul, MN: Llewellyn, 1990.

Fogel, Edwin M. *Beliefs and Superstitions of the Pennsylvania Germans*. Philadelphia: American Germanica Press, 1915.

Frater U.˙.D.˙. *Practical Sigil Magic*. St. Paul, MN: Llewellyn, 1990.

Gandee, Lee R. *Strange Experience*. Englewood Cliffs, NJ: Prentice Hall, 1971.

Hohman, John George. *Der lange verborgene Freund*. Reading, PA: The author, [1819?] (Numerous reprints and translations)

Hollander, Lee M., trans. *The Poetic Edda*. Austin. TX: University of Texas Press, 1962.

Jung, Carl G. "Wotan." In: *The Collected Works*. Princeton: University of Princeton Press, 1964 Vol 10, pp. 179-193.

Lewis, Arthur H. *Hex*. New York: Trident, 1969.

List, Guido von. *The Secret of the Runes*. Translated by Stephen E. Flowers. Rochester, VT: Destiny Books, 1988.

Sturluson, Snorri. *The Prose Edda*. Translated by A.G. Brodeur. New York: The Scandinavian American Foundation, 1929.

Thorsson, Edred. *Futhark: A Handbook of Rune Magic*. York Beach, ME: Weiser, 1984.

————. *Runelore: A Handbook of Esoteric Runology*. York Beach, ME: Weiser, 1987.

————. *At the Well of Wyrd: A Handbook of Runic Divination*. York Beach, ME: Weiser, 1988

————. *Rune Might: Secret Practices of the German Rune Magicians.* St. Paul, MN: Llewellyn, 1989.

————. *The Nine Doors of Midgard.* St. Paul, MN: Llewellyn, 1991.

Turville-Petre, E. O. G. *Myth and Religion of the North.* New York: Holt Rinehart & Winston, 1964.

STAY IN TOUCH

On the following pages you will find listed, with their current prices, some of the books now available on related subjects. Your book dealer stocks most of these, and will stock new titles in the Llewellyn series as they become available. We urge your patronage.

To obtain a FREE COPY of our latest full CATALOG of New Age books, tapes, videos, products and services, just write to the address below. In each 80-page catalog sent out bimonthly, you will find articles, reviews, the latest information on New Age topics, a listing of news and events, and much more. It is an exciting and informative way to stay in touch with the New Age and the world. The first copy will be sent free of charge and you will continue receiving copies as long as you are an active customer. You may also subscribe to *The Llewellyn New Times* by sending a $5.00 donation ($20.00 for overseas). Order your copy of *The Llewellyn New Times* today!

The Llewellyn New Times
P.O. Box 64383-Dept. 782, St. Paul, MN 55164

TO ORDER BOOKS AND PRODUCTS ON THE FOLLOWING PAGES:

If your book dealer does not carry the titles listed on the following pages, you may order them directly from Llewellyn. Please send full price in U.S. funds, plus $1.50 for postage and handling for orders *under* $10.00; $3.00 for orders *over* $10.00. There are no postage and handling charges for orders over $50. UPS Delivery: We ship UPS whenever possible. Delivery guaranteed. Provide your street address as UPS does not deliver to P.O. Boxes; UPS to Canada requires a $50 minimum order. Allow 4-6 weeks for delivery. Orders outside the USA and Canada: Airmail—add retail price of book; add $5 for each non-book item (tapes, etc.); add $1 per item for surface mail. You may use your major credit card to order these titles by calling 1-800-THE-MOON, M-F, 8:00-5:00, Central Time. Send orders to:

LLEWELLYN PUBLICATIONS
P.O. BOX 64383-782
St. Paul, MN 55164-0383, U.S.A.

THE NINE DOORS OF MIDGARD
by Edred Thorsson

The Nine Doors of Midgard are the gateways to self-transformation through the runes. This is the complete course of study and practice which has successfully been in use inside the Rune-Gild for ten years. Now it is being made available to the public for the first time.

The runic tradition is the northern or Teutonic equivalent of the Hermetic tradition of the south. *The Nine Doors of Midgard* is the only manual to take a systematic approach to initiation into runic practices.

Through nine "lessons" or stages in a graded curriculum, the books takes the rune student from a stage in which no previous knowledge of runes or esoteric work is assumed to a fairly advanced stage of initiation. The book also contains a complete reading course in outside material.

0-87542-781-2, 336 pgs., illus., softcover $12.95

A BOOK OF TROTH
by Edred Thorsson

One of the most widespread of the ancient pagan revivals is Asatru or Odinism. Its followers seek to rekindle the way of the North, of the ancient Teutonic peoples. Until now, no book has completely expressed the nature and essence of that movement. *A Book of Troth* is that book.

This is the most traditional and well-informed general guide to the practice of the elder Germanic folk way. The official document of the organization known simply as the "Ring of Troth," *A Book of Troth* is not a holy book or bible in the usual sense. Rather it outlines a code of behavior and a set of actions, not a doctrine or a way of believing.

A Book of Troth presents for the first time the essence of Teutonic neopaganism between two covers. It is a must for anyone interested in an effective system based on ancient and timeless principles.

0-87542-777-4, 248 pgs., illus., softcover $9.95

RUNE MIGHT:
Secret Practices of the German Rune Magicians
by Edred Thorsson

Rune Might reveals, for the first time in the English language, the long-hidden secrets of the German rune magicians who practiced their arts in the beginning of the century. By studying the contents of *Rune Might* and working with the exercises, the reader will be able to experience the direct power of the runes as experienced by the Early German rune magicians.

The exercises represent bold new methods of drawing magical power into your life—regardless of the magical tradition or system with which you normally work. No other system does this in quite the direct and clearly defined ways that rune exercises do.

0-87542-778-2, 192 pgs., 5 1/4 x 8, illus., softcover   **$7.95**

FIRE & ICE
by S. Edred Flowers

The hidden beliefs and practices of German occultism have long held a strong fascination for the poet as well as the historian. The greatest of the German secret lodges—the Fraternitas Saturni—revealed neither its membership, its beliefs, nor its rites. Through a chance occurrence, the inner documents of this order were recently published in Germany. *Fire & Ice* is the first study of these documents to be published in any language. This book relates the fascinating histories of the founders and leaders of the Fraternitas Saturni. You will witness the development of its magical beliefs and practices, its banishment by the Nazi government, and its many postwar dissensions and conflicts. The Saturnian path of initiation is revealed in full detail, and the magical formulas which are included can be used for your own self-development as well as for more practical and concrete goals.

0-87542-776-6, 5114 x 8, 240 pgs., illus., softcover   **$9.95**

TEUTONIC MAGIC
The Magical & Spiritual Practices
of the Germanic Peoples
by Kveldulf Gundarsson

The word "Teutonic," once used exclusively to denote a specific German tribe, now encompasses a heritage as large and varied as Northern Europe. In *Teutonic Magic*, Kveldulf Gundarsson presents the theory and practice of Teutonic magic, a style of magic of particular interest to anyone of Northern European descent.

The focus of the book is primarily on the Elder Futhark, the magical rune alphabet. Gundarsson explains runic divination, rune magic, rituals for carving rune-tines and more. There is also a considerable amount of information on Teutonic ritual practice and the Teutonic worlds, gods and spirits. This book is perfect for those of Northern European ancestry seeking to recover their heritage.

0-87542-291-8, 311 pgs., 6 x 9, illus., softcover $12.95

LEAVES OF YGGDRASIL
by Freya Aswynn

Leaves of Yggdrasil is the first book to offer an extensive presentation of Rune concepts, mythology and magical applications inspired by Dutch/Frisian traditional lore.

Author Freya Aswynn, although writing from a historical perspective, offers her own interpretations of this data based on her personal experience with the system.

Leaves of Yggdrasil emphasizes the feminine mysteries and the function of the Northern priestesses. It unveils a complete and personal system of the rune magic that will fascinate students of mythology, spirituality, psychism and Teutonic history, for this is not only a religious autobiography but also a historical account of the ancient Northern European culture.

0-87542-024-9, 5-1/4 x 8, 304 pgs., softcover $12.95

NORSE MAGIC
by D. J. Conway

The Norse—adventurous Viking wanderers, daring warriors, worshipers of the Aesir and the Vanir. Like the Celtic tribes, the Northmen had strong ties with the Earth and Elements, the Gods and the "little people."

The book leads the beginner step by step through the spells. The in-depth discussion of Norse deities and the Norse way of life and worship set the intermediate student on the path to developing his or her own active rituals.

Norse Magic is a compelling and easy-to-read introduction to the Norse religion and Teutonic mythology. The magical techniques are refreshingly direct and simple, with a strong feminine and goddess orientation.

0-87542-137-7, 240 pgs., mass market, illus. **$3.95**

CELTIC MAGIC
by D. J. Conway

Many people, not all of Irish descent, have a great interest in the ancient Celts and the Celtic pantheon, and *Celtic Magic* is the map they need for exploring this ancient and fascinating magical culture.

Celtic Magic is for the reader who is either a beginner or intermediate in the field of magic, providing an extensive "how-to" of practical spell-working. There are many books on the market dealing with the Celts and their beliefs, but none guide the reader to a practical application of magical knowledge for use in everyday life. There is also an in-depth discussion of Celtic deities and the Celtic way of life and worship, so that an intermediate practitioner can expand upon the spellwork to build a series of magical rituals. Presented in an easy-to-understand format.

Celtic Magic is for anyone searching for new spells that can be worked immediately, without elaborate or rare materials, and with minimal time and preparation.

0-87542-136-9, 240 pgs., mass market, illus. **$3.95**